Praying *for*
That Man

PRAYING *for* THAT MAN

A Love Story *from Above*

LEANNE ROZELL

with Malary Hill
Genevieve V. Georget
and Sarah Byrd

Writers of the Round Table Press
PO Box 1603, Deerfield, IL 60015
www.roundtablecompanies.com

Editors: *Malary Hill, Genevieve V. Georget, Sarah Byrd*
Cover Designer: *Christy Bui*
Interior Designer: *Christy Bui*
Proofreaders: *Adam Lawrence, Carly Cohen*

Printed in the United States of America

First Edition: November 2020
10 9 8 7 6 5 4 3 2 1

Library of Congress Cataloging-in-Publication Data
Rozell, Leanne.
Praying for that man: a love story from above
/ Leanne Rozell.—1st ed. p. cm.
ISBN Paperback: 978-1-61066-090-7
ISBN Digital: 978-1-61066-091-4
ISBN Audiobook: 978-1-61066-092-1
Library of Congress Control Number: 2020918298

Writers of the Round Table Press and the logo
are trademarks of Writers of the Round Table, Inc.

This book is dedicated to my God, who is the author and perfecter of my faith. This is HIS story in my life.

Prologue

I once read a story about a girl with a red umbrella.

The story is told of a time when a small community was experiencing a drought. It had lasted for some time and the farmers were struggling. As the problem became worse, a local priest called a prayer meeting to ask for rain. Many people showed up for the gathering, and as the priest walked the aisle, his eyes scanned the crowd in admiration of his community's faithfulness. When he reached the front of the church, he noticed a young girl—about eleven years old—sitting quietly in the front row, her face beaming with excitement. Next to her, poised and ready for use, was a bright red umbrella. No one else in the congregation had brought an umbrella. All came to pray for rain, but the little girl came *expecting* rain.

Our journey with the Lord is about becoming the girl with the red umbrella. It's about not just saying our prayers but about *knowing* that God will answer them.

Please believe that my desire for you is to have a relationship with God and to understand who He is and who He is not. He is not a genie in a bottle. He is not a bearded man living in the North Pole. He created heaven and earth, and He is bigger than any of us can even imagine, and so are His answers to our prayers.

• • •

When I began to write this book, I wanted everyone's story to be like mine. But what I have learned through laying out my life on these pages is that everyone's story is unique and perfect in its own way. My story won't match yours. But God isn't into carbon copies. He is the Creator of individual masterpieces. The point is, we all have a love story. Because regardless of what we desire for ourselves, God is passionate about pursuing us and our hearts.

I pray you do not miss out on the love story that God has for you. And my hope for your future is that you will see that when we put the King first, there's always room for a prince in our lives.

I guess what I'm trying to say is this:

Pray.

Then grab an umbrella, child … because you're going to need it.

With love,
Leanne

One

Shadows in the Dark

Once upon a time in a faraway land,
there was a tiny kingdom.

—*Cinderella*[1]

L IKE ALL GOOD LOVE STORIES, mine began with a boy falling in love with a girl.

My parents met in the small Texas town of Stanford, a re-
mote farming community with red dirt, cotton fields, wind-
mills, and not much else. However, unlike cotton, you don't
need rain for love to bloom. And so my parents' love began
in the unripe years of seventh grade. My dad, the all-Ameri-
can athlete, and my mom, the good Southern girl, were married before they were even done with their freshman year
of college. At eighteen years old, their challenges may have
run wide, but their love for each other ran deep. And eventually, this love led them to Big Spring, Texas, where both of
my parents taught math and my father became a golf and
football coach.

After seven years of just the two of them, my older brother, Marcus, was born, and only fifteen months later, they
had a baby girl. When I was only two, we moved into our new
home in a small Texas town named Graham. This faraway

---

1   All references to the film come from the following version: *Cinderella*
    (Burbank, CA: Walt Disney Productions, 1950), directed by Clyde Geronimi,
    Wilfred Jackson, and Hamilton Luske, 74 min.

land became the tiny kingdom I grew up in, and it oozed with the small-town Texas "Howdy, y'all" charm. Tucked away about 120 miles west of Dallas, Graham actually peaked in its population when I was in my early teens at around nine thousand people. Its quiet isolation never seemed unusual to us. When it's the only place you experience, it becomes the only experience you know. For years, I had only ever seen movies on a big screen at a drive-in theater. We would pile into our dad's pickup truck and head to the giant field only a few miles from our house, the dirt ground blowing up dust as all of the cars settled in around us. We'd hang the brick-sized speaker on the side of the truck window and sit back to watch *Star Wars: Episode VI—Return of the Jedi* on the large outdoor screen while the mosquitoes ate away at us in the deep Texas heat. In a lot of ways, our drive-in was more of a social occasion for our community, people bringing lawn chairs and gathering together to catch up on the time that went by. Teenagers tried to sneak in friends, and kids played with one another in the field. Graham was also a dry county, only beginning to sell wine and beer within the county lines in 2017. Up until then, any person wanting to wet their whistle would have to drive to the lone liquor store at the edge of town in no-man's-land and bring back the forbidden fruit. In many ways, Graham really was a little piece of shelter in a rather unruly world.

From church to school to shopping, we lived in a bubble where everyone knew each other. My mother remained a schoolteacher and was always our biggest cheerleader. My father, still a high school coach, constantly infused our lives with playfulness and laughter. My brother was my best friend from birth, my protector, and my confidant. In Graham, we didn't measure the passage of time the way most communities would.

While the seasonal weather would pass over most towns, bringing cooler air and a change of colors, Graham's annual clock ticked to the sound of football season and school bells ringing. In preparation for this season's approach, we would drive an hour north to Wichita Falls—the closest metropolitan city—with a list in hand and purpose in mind. We made each one of these seasonal trips an event, attempting all of our clothes shopping for the next six months and making sure to indulge in "fine" dining at one of the mall's many food court restaurants. Bringing our "big city" memories home filled our hearts with excitement and allowed us to hold on until the next round of necessities would set a new date on the calendar. Graham moved to its own rhythm, and those of us who lived there were happy to beat along to the drum.

But regardless of where you lived in Texas, there was one thing we all agreed upon, and that was our commitment to two things: Jesus and football. And not necessarily in that order. Texans bleed team colors, and if you lived in Graham, you were playing football, coaching football, or watching football. And as for Sundays, well, you knew where to find us then too: heading to church the way most would head to a country club. At least three Sundays out of every month, my mom, Marcus, and I would pile into our van, wearing our Sunday best, and head off to First Baptist Church. Yes, we were drawn to church by our deep love of God, but we were also drawn there because it never really occurred to us not to be. Being a Christian in Texas is like being born into a royal family: it's part of your DNA, and the bloodline is strong. There does come a time, though, when you've gone through the motions long enough, and you catch yourself thinking: it's hard to be found if you've never been lost.

Our lives in Graham were spent in a little ranch-style house off Wolf Road, with a basketball hoop attached to the garage door and brown siding that ran along the walls. With the house surrounded by bluffs, mesquite trees, and open spaces, my brother and I tackled the wilderness like Mowgli tackled the jungle. In creek beds and tree branches, our tanned skin and dirty nails became the fingerprints of our latest adventures. And when we weren't riding our skateboards or bikes down the driveway, hitting golf balls into the yard, or chasing each other to exhaustion, we had our own rhythms that played out each day. We'd wake up each morning, scramble through the cupboards to find our own breakfast, and lay our chosen spread out on our painted baby blue TV trays in our living room. The morning hustle always whispered in the background: my mom, humming as she put on her liquid eyeliner, and my dad, sometimes loading our van in the driveway out front and sometimes already gone with his school bus driver duties, which started far earlier than my morning wake-up call.

A gentle knock on my bedroom door would let me know that it was time to start the day, and I would shuffle down our long hallway in my Garfield nightshirt to debate whether I should have cereal or leftover chocolate cake for breakfast. Oddly enough, my parents didn't seem to mind either way what I ate. As long as it was easy and convenient, it had to be good. Boxed food and canned goods with expiration dates lasting for years was how Betty Crocker taught my mom that she didn't have to spend hours in the kitchen to feed her family. Growing up hearing that cake was just as good as a doughnut made breakfast an easy choice for Marcus and I.

School days also brought with them a pulse all their own. Walking out the door of our home, Strawberry Shortcake lunchbox in hand, and, let's be honest, probably more cake inside the lunchbox, I would run to our large tan-and-brown van, hop into my seat, and eagerly dream about the events of that day that awaited me at Woodland Elementary School.

In a small town like ours, school was the central hub of social events and play. With little hands clutching a book and folders, we would run into school, wave to the teacher waiting to greet us at the front door, and make our way down the long corridor to our prospective classrooms. Marcus, in his true nature, would drop me off at my classroom with a smile and wave of assurance. I would hang my lunchbox on my designated hook, plant myself in my assigned chair, and prepare to take in all that the day had to offer me. For the most part, I loved school. My favorite subjects were math and physical education. I loved gym class mostly because I was good at it and could, oftentimes, out-jump anyone in the jump rope contests. Math was a favorite because numbers made sense to me and, well, I didn't have to spell. The only true dread of my day was English, as it exposed one of my biggest insecurities: my struggle with reading.

Ever since I can remember, I had always felt like I was different, especially when I attempted to pick up a book. Since my parents were teachers, they also saw the signs of my struggle, and, when I was around eight years old, they decided to take me to the Scottish Rite Hospital in Dallas to have me tested for a learning disability. After numerous tests, the doctors explained to my parents that I had dyslexia. At the time, there were many misconceptions about dyslexia and what this meant for the person who had it. And because of these misconceptions, my parents were told I would never read for pleasure, that school would always be a challenge, and with my severe case I would not make it in college.

My parents wanted to give me my best chance, so upon diagnosis, they shared this information with the school, hoping that they could offer some guidance and support. However, due to limited resources and understanding of dyslexia, the school I attended did not know what to do with me, so I was placed in the learning-disabled class with students that were mentally and physically disabled. Many of these children were in wheelchairs, could not feed themselves, and required the constant attention and supervision of an adult to keep them safe. And while I am thankful that there was a place for these children, my eight-year-old self was scared, confused, and desperately wanting to get out of this classroom that felt so foreign to me. I decided that I was going to do whatever was necessary to change my situation at school, and so I came home one day and, with my arms crossed over my chest, told my mother that I would not go back to that class under any circumstances. I demanded that she was to never tell anyone I had dyslexia. I told her I would not let my difficulty with spelling and reading stop me in school, that I could do everything the other kids were doing, and that I would just have to try harder.

While my determined resilience might have surprised her initially, my mom, who was dedicated to seeing me succeed, immediately pulled me out of the disabled class and had me reassigned to my old classroom. She promised that she would help me to achieve my goals by helping me understand the symbols of the written word. She never broke that promise.

While days ebbed and flowed inside of the school building, I could always count on recess to provide endless excitement, energy, and adventure. I loved to play, and as the afternoon heat began to warm the ground outside of our school, we would run to grab the prime spots on the playground. My friends and I spent hours of time each week swinging our tiny little bodies across the monkey bars, hanging by our legs, or battling one another through endless rounds of Red Rover. Everything seemed full of possibility out there. The wide-open spaces and the sun's bright light helped me to push through any fears, frustrations, or doubts that crept in while engulfed in the large brick building that loomed in the background.

Eventually, day would lead to night, and we would find ourselves right back where we began: our home, our family, our rhythm. Most times, Marcus and I would head outside and back into the woods until it was time for dinner. But other times, I couldn't resist getting lost in fairy tales. Cinderella was always my favorite. The animals. The singing. The magical pursuit of it all. What girl doesn't want to leave an impression that her handsome prince can't live without? What person doesn't want to be seen for their truest selves and loved beyond their torn exteriors?

I adored fairy tales the way any young girl was captivated by a good love story. But I also catch myself wondering now, as an adult, if there isn't a danger in waiting to be rescued, to be found, to be seen by this unknown prince. If there isn't danger in waiting for the perfect human to save us and slay all of the dragons in our lives. Being pursued by another person seems like perfection, but this expectation of any one flawed human is a lot to ask. But still, as a child, I dreamed of beautiful transformations, that handsome prince and a happily-ever-after. And this is what I carried with me down the hall each night as the sun set along the horizon and I prepared to drift off for another day.

My bedroom had orange shag carpet and a time-worn four-poster bed set in the middle of the room, handed down to me from my grandmother. I think that my bedroom held a lot of the same things as most other girls my age did: posters on the walls, flowers on the blankets, dreams in our hearts.

At that time, we were still young enough to be wrapped up in innocent bliss but old enough to know that the entire world still awaited us. Bedtime, though, was always a force to be reckoned with. There was just something about the way the world felt once the lights went out that always seemed to remind me that I was never really alone. But then there was that light that came from my closet. It's those tiny streaks of light that I remember most. The way they would glow across my bedroom floor and, in their own subtle way, bring comfort in the night. Looking back, it's amazing to think about how much security can be found from a single light bulb. Later in life, I would find many other ways to distract myself from the scared and restless feelings that would go bump in the night, but when I was eight years old, this was it. My door would be closed and our house would be silent, but with the click of a switch, that light—gently streaming through the shutter like doors of my childhood closet—managed to chase away all of the dark shadows that tried to swallow me whole.

Except for one night.

I don't know what most other little girls would do when evil literally moves through their space and disrupts their sense of security, but as for me, I was filled with fear—fear that this presence would take me, and fear that it would change me. And as this shadow moved across my room and onto the wall where the four photos hung, a feeling of horror filled my body in the most inexplicable way. Even as a child, I knew with certainty this was more than a mere darkening of light. This darkness was tangibly real; it was from beyond. As my breath quickened and my heart beat rapidly inside of my chest, I gripped onto the edge of my light pink covers and pulled them up closer to my face. My little body was frozen still as all of the blood in my body rushed quickly to my brain, trying to help it make sense of what was happening in front of my eyes. And as this shadow figure stopped, they moved. The pictures moved. The four little girl pictures were arranged on the wall like a compass, each one set as the cardinal points. The orientation of the girl with the blue bonnet was displayed as north, the girl with the yellow sunflowers as east, the girl with the red umbrella as south, and the girl in a pink bathtub with bubbles floating all around as west. And now right beside them on the wall was the shadow. Then each one slowly switched spots on the wall, turning like a clock and gently placing themselves back onto the wall.

Now this dark visitor had me in his grasp, and I could feel its presence deep within my bones. Leaving the safety of my closet light behind, I retreated to the fetal position in the middle of my mattress, allowing my sweaty little hands to clench the blankets and pull them tightly over my head. I covered myself completely, attempting to shield my body from the crippling fear that enveloped my mind, the fear that came from knowing that my space of comfort had become a space of distress. And now, utterly alone in this space, I was left unsure of what to do next. I had an inkling to call out to my parents but wondered if they would even believe me. I still wondered if I believed it. And so I did the only thing that I thought I had left to do.

I prayed.

For the first time that I can remember, I called out to God and begged Him to stop the evil that was planted in my room. At that age I had a deep feeling that God was bigger and stronger than anything, and since that was absolute in my young mind, He would take care of me. I cried and I prayed, and when I slowly came out from beneath my hiding place, it was over. The shadow was gone, but the images remained in their new place. Looking at those pictures was a solid reminder that dark forces move among us. I awoke the next morning, and for the thirty-five years that followed, I would never speak a word of the dark shadow I experienced that night and the manner in which God saved me from it.

When you're little, you don't wonder about the future and the decisions that you'll have to make. You play outside with your brother and watch your mom cook dinner in the microwave and learn about football. But this night was the beginning. It was the beginning of discovering the forces at play in this world. It was the beginning of realizing that, sometimes, life is a battle, and you can either be victorious or lie among the trenches in defeat. And it was the beginning of understanding that, despite it all, my once-upon-a-time story started with an unseen Hero who was there to ensure that I was never alone.

Two
An Invitation to Joy

> You don't have time to be timid.
> You must be bold, daring.
>
> *—Beauty and the Beast*[2]

I N OUR LITTLE TOWN, neighborhood kids often found themselves intertwined in friendship by proximity. My lucky
draw was a girl my age named Amanda, who lived three
doors down and in so many ways was everything that I didn't
know myself to be. She wore expensive shoes and jelly bracelets halfway up her arm. She carried herself with a certain
self-assurance that I didn't possess, and her lively personality
felt as though it took up all of the oxygen in the room. She
was the girly girl to my tomboy. She was the cool kid to my
messy adventures. She was the confidence to my uncertainty.

I met Amanda when I was three, and at that age we were
inseparable. However, as time passed, the dynamics of our relationship began to change. While the two of us began to grow
and find our place in the world, the innocence of our infant
relationship began to shift as well, and slowly but steadily she
began to dominate our relationship. Part of it was because
she took control, and part of it was because I let her. I can remember sitting in my bedroom, writing journal entries about
the day, always centering my feelings and experiences on

---

2   *Beauty and the Beast* (Burbank, CA: Walt Disney Pictures, 1991), directed
     by Gary Trousdale and Kirk Wise, 84 min.

Amanda: whether or not she would play with me or talk to me or find time in her day to acknowledge the human in me. Our relationship during our preteen years would be best described as a teeter-totter of emotions. One day, I would feel on top of the world, beaming at the experience of being seen by her, and the next I would be sitting to the side, merely an observer as she shone brightly on someone else. In my mind, there was no such thing as a level playing field with Amanda. I wanted her to like me, and somehow, over the course of time, I had allowed her to dictate my worth and my value and my joy on any given day, which meant that I was constantly swinging on a pendulum that only Amanda controlled.

We do this as people sometimes. We hinge our acceptance on what someone else thinks of us and then wonder why we feel shaky, faltering, and unsteady instead of enjoying the feeling of comfortably standing on solid ground.

My relationship with Amanda finally brought me to the end of myself one afternoon when I confided in her. Earlier that day, I had taken my mom's pink sponge rollers and cut them in half. I remember playing with the pink foam curlers in the bathroom. I remember taking out the hair scissors from the drawer and thinking that I could trim up these curlers the same way I trimmed up my own bangs. I cut one side and then the other, but just like my bangs, once one side is shorter than the other, the seesaw keeps teetering back and forth until there is just a pile of pink pieces.

This act was out of character for me, and as the broken pieces sat on the counter, I suddenly felt this surge of panic at the fear of getting caught. I knew I had ruined something that didn't belong to me, and I knew that I couldn't put it back together. I also knew the only way to keep this a secret was to hide what I had just done. And so I did what any little kid would do: I quickly dug my hands to the bottom of the trash-can, threw the cut-up pieces to the bottom, and tossed the remaining garbage over the evidence of my sin. For a moment, I almost felt a sense of security in my decision. My problem was solved, my sin was hidden.

It's funny how sins of the past linger in our hearts, finding a way to reappear, exposing us all over again. My little heart was so riddled with the guilt and shame over what I had just done that the only way to relieve the tension in my soul was to tell someone. So on that same day, I decided to confide in Amanda. However, in that moment, my plan to gain comfort quickly turned, and rather than console me, she used this as an opportunity to gain leverage and use my vulnerability against me.

"Take off all your clothes and run down the driveway all the way to the road and back, buck naked," she commanded "or I will tell your mom exactly what you did."

As the words dripped from her mouth, I felt shocked at her request. Then, seeing she was serious, I felt stuck. The dry Texas air began to fill my lungs, and as she grinned at the control she knew she had over me, I stood paralyzed in a moment that I now felt I couldn't get out of. Amanda knew I had to decide between the wrath of my parents and the embarrassment of a run down the driveway, baring my naked body to her and anyone else who happened to pass by. I was afraid, I was panicked, I was uncertain, and my fear was tangible to her. As a ten-year-old girl, I was terrified to tell my mom that I had cut her pink sponge curlers. Standing there in the driveway, questions whirling through my mind, I tried to make sense of what was happening and what I should do.

How much could pink sponge curlers possibly cost?

Ten dollars?
One hundred dollars?
How did I end up here?
Why did I cut those stupid curlers?

The truth was that I didn't know why I did it, and now I didn't want to admit my guilt at having done it. I believed that if I wanted to keep the curlers a secret, to protect the relationship I had with my mom and keep it unscathed, I would have to decide: fear or shame? So I decided to hand over my dignity in exchange for the safekeeping of my mother-daughter relationship.

Somehow, at this age, there seemed more security in this decision. And so, piece-by-piece, I took off my clothes—each item forming a pile on the pavement beneath my feet. Now I was entirely exposed. Naked. A feeling of unbridled vulnerability flooding my entire being. I realized, standing fully exposed in front of her, that my feelings of panic and fear were far greater than they had been earlier on when my secret was all my own. Now I had nothing to protect me. Not only had she learned my secret, but she had found a way to take away my dignity. She had conquered me. And as my shirt hit the ground, my body shaking in cowardly dread, amazement spread across Amanda's face as she watched it all happen.

Quickly, my feet charged out from under me. My little, naked body dashed from the concrete slab near our garage door, doing all that it could to just complete the task and end the shame that followed with each passing step. Just like the dirt flying out from beneath my bare feet, my innocence felt as though it was being tossed into the wind, being sacrificed, disappearing forever in a cloud of dust behind me. And as the earth settled beneath me at the end of my long run of shame, I looked up at Amanda, whose face, once authoritative, quickly shifted as she turned her head. In a mere second, her confident smile turned to cowardice as a booming voice sternly ordered her to head home. And as her eyes fell from me, fearfully running away, I saw the giant figure of my father turn toward me and, pointing toward the house, command my obedience to get inside and get dressed.

"Get in the house, Leanne. Now!" he yelled, as my eyes quickly lowered to the ground. I flew past him with my shoulders hunched and my spirit wounded trying to hide my shame.

The rest of my day was spent on our old orange couch, accompanied by the only comfort that would come: my tears. I bawled. The experience of being exposed, being caught, running through my mind for hours on that couch. While lying there, hoping for the consolation of words, I stared angrily out the window across from me. The sky that day was a beautiful blue, filled with perfectly fluffy white clouds. What would ordinarily be a welcome sight filled me with frustration and heartache. I hated the sky for not echoing my internal turmoil and gloom. I wanted the sky to tell my story, the story no one seemed to want to hear. I wanted the sky to reflect my sorrow and cry, to open its floodgates and weep for me. I so desperately wanted my parents to hear my side of the story, to come to me and ask what happened, to want to help console me in my grief. But all day long, as my heart ached to be seen, my parents avoided me.

Eventually, after hours of agonizing frustration, I burst into the kitchen and shared the story of *why* I bared myself to Amanda and the rest of the neighborhood. I confessed to my mom that I had cut her curlers, that I was scared of what would happen if I told her, and that Amanda used that story against me. But there was a shift ... now the confession was my ally, and as all of my fears poured out of my mouth, they were caught, ever so gently, by my mother's compassionate heart. She crouched down, she listened, and she loved me, telling me that the curlers' value was nothing compared to mine. Confession brought restoration, not destruction.

I was loved. I was seen. I was forgiven.

I would like to say that my mother's love and understanding helped me to see myself and my true value differently. I also would like to say that things changed between Amanda and I after this incident, but, to be honest, so much stayed the same. I still longed for her friendship, and she knew it. So after about a week or so, all was forgotten. And this deep desire to feel seen and validated would become a pattern that would follow me throughout my teenage and young adult years: yearning, always, to feel valued, and willing, always, to hand a piece of myself over in exchange for it.

I didn't realize it then, but I understand now that my dad, by catching me in this act of shame, opened the door for the truth to come out.

Fatherhood was my dad's calling. He eased into his role as parent like scoring a touchdown, celebration dance and all. My dad still is incredibly fun-loving, and his enthusiasm over games was contagious. In fact, I am pretty sure that is where I got my playfulness and competitive nature.

Everything we did together could be made into a spirited contest, and nothing—not a rainy day, bad mood, or sickness—could shut down the fun. On many occasions, Marcus and I could be found hitting golf balls in the backyard, our dad cheering us on to hit it "just a little bit farther" like he often did coaching me on the golf course, or running down the hall, flipping over mountains of pillows, always pushing our boundaries with some new challenge.

That's one thing I remember so clearly. The celebration. He celebrated us! He celebrated every victory, and he had a strategic plan after every loss. Coaching and parenting were one and the same for my dad, and it made for a "never a dull moment" kind of childhood.

Six days out of the week my dad was the coach, but on Sunday mornings mom rallied the troops. Every single week, she marched my brother and I from our home to the First Baptist Church. And as Marcus and I would head into our Sunday school class, my mom made her way to the sanctuary.

This classroom looked like any other—with a blackboard on the wall and a teacher who led us through crafts with sticky white glue and dried macaroni while reading the story of "Noah and the Ark." I loved that we would be rewarded with gold stars for remembering Bible verses and that we were encouraged to sing and dance loudly and enthusiastically. There was so much joy in this space, and as we sang, our tiny voices could be heard all the way down the hall. But as all good things tend to do, Sunday school would come to an end, and we would get sent back to the wide-open space that was our sanctuary or "Big Church." This was where the colorful stories I heard just an hour before became a dull and boring drawl. I would often daydream as I sat in the pews with my mom, while my feet, donned with Mary Janes and frilly lace socks, swung back and forth under the big wooden pew like two flowers trying to escape eternal boredom.

To be honest, church often seemed like more of a ritual than a learning opportunity to me. Its structure caused me to get caught up in the monotony of the message, the routine of the altar call, the repetitiveness of the songs. I would look around Big Church with stained glass windows reflecting colors on the wall, and the room full of faces looking for hope, seeking redemption, desiring comfort, and yet I often found my-self thinking only about how I could speed the message along.

That is until I saw her.

I can't remember the day, I can't remember the time, but I can remember her face and the radiant light that seemed to illuminate from it. It was obvious to me that she was older than a teenager but not as old as my mother, and I was completely captivated. Her dark hair and fair skin made her look like Snow White, and I was sure if she started singing, little furry animals would come scampering to her side. But she didn't walk out of a fairy-tale movie. She was real, and she added life and beauty to the space just by being in it. However, something else made her stand out of the crowd, something beyond her beautiful exterior. I didn't know what to call it except to say that she had a glow. In my young heart, I knew that I wanted whatever it was she had. With boldness, I asked her what it was that gave her such radiance or, in my simple words, her glow.

"I have Jesus inside of me. I love Him, and He makes me smile. That's what you see, sweet girl. You see joy."

Jesus gave her joy.

That joy made her glow.

And with those words, time seemed to slow down, and my awareness shifted to the space that surrounded me. Suddenly, this place that so often felt unknown to me seemed so full of life and power, and my heart, at age ten, was filled with a surety that I had not encountered before. I knew that if I wanted to experience that joy, that radiant glow, then I wanted to love Jesus as much as she did. So I prayed. And this prayer was the beginning of Him boldly entering into my life, walking alongside me through each step and stumble but, most of all, making sure that I would never be the same.

After this initial encounter, I was radically zealous for Jesus. I was so excited to know Him and longed to serve Him in any way that I could. I loved Him. Unashamedly, unconditionally, wholly, I loved Him, and I wanted everyone to know it. This childlike love also dug its tiny roots into my prayer life, and I have carried this immense love and trust to this day. I believed fully that He would not only hear my prayers but answer each and every one of them. And so I would pray. And each time He would answer my prayer, I would jot the date down in my red notebook as proof of His goodness. Proof of His faithfulness. Proof Jesus loved me. And proof I loved Him. I trusted that God would guide my path. My Heavenly Father found me, and He not only supported me but He became my strong foundation, even in the moments where it seemed that the walls were crumbling around me.

Three
That Guy

Even miracles take a little time.
—*Cinderella*

EVERYONE ALWAYS LIKES THE SCENE WITH THE GLASS SLIP-PER THE MOST. That beautiful moment when the prince places the lost slipper on Cinderella's foot and the kingdom finally knows she's the one. But I always liked the moment *before* that: the moment when she walks down the staircase, in her ragged dress and messy hair. I loved how she confidently held the wooden banister and stood tall in the person she was after midnight. I loved how the prince looked up at her and knew. He *knew*. He knew by the look in her eye, and he knew by the grace in her step. He knew even before she tried the slipper on that she was the one. There's just something about that moment that has stuck with me all these years; the pursuit through the kingdom, knocking on every door, searching for the one he knew he was meant to find.

The glass slipper was about the rest of the world.

But that silent moment, as she walked down the stairs, their eyes locked on one another: *that* was about just the two of them.

I think that true love is a hard thing for any child to understand. The idea of living out one's life with someone and choosing that one right person to walk alongside is complicated at the best of times, all the more so for young minds. But there does come a time when you look around and, like the story of "Noah's Ark" that I learned in my little church classroom, the world is paired up in twos. In time, I began to realize that I also wanted to be one-half of a pair. I wanted to have a companion, someone who saw me, knew me, and loved me. Like a collage of images placed on a piece of poster board, I flipped through the pages of the couples I saw and cut out my favorite parts, pasting them in my mind for the future patiently awaiting me.

My parents showed me commitment and loyalty. They were married at a young age and are still married to this day. They have been a remarkable example of what it means to remain steadfast through love and challenges and years of witnessing one another's lives. They showed me what it meant to raise children and work hard and move forward in a common direction for the good of our entire family. It was and continues to be a marriage that works for them, and in observing their union, I pulled out the qualities that I admired most, taking note of the strengths that made my parents the pillars of stability that my brother and I knew them to be. So I mentally took my pair of scissors and pasted their qualities into a spiral notebook as I conspired to create my own fairy-tale story.

Then there was the youth pastor and his wife, the one who shared her love of Jesus with me. I would watch them every Sunday at church and notice the subtleties of their own marriage that were so different from the ones I noticed at home. There was a deep sense of adoration in their love for one another, and I was enchanted by its intimacy. I noticed it in the way he always brought her into the conversation they were having. It was in the way he would gently place his hand on her lower back to let her know that he was right there. It was in the way they would look at each other from across the room. It was in the gentleness of their voices and the attentiveness of their words. It was in the caring, the respect, the devotion, and the desire that permeated whatever space they entered together.

My parents' love was a weathered one. It had been through storms, endured many years, and settled into a rhythm that could be described as nothing but admirable. The youth pastor's love, on the other hand, was new and fresh. It was filled with promise and a future of many years out in front of them. It was exciting and delicate and a story still very much in the making. So I took those beautiful pieces and added them to my creation, to the vision of what my own love would look like. Like excavating a site with buried treasure, I was unearthing all of the things I loved most about marriage in hopes of one day claiming each of them as my own.

But for all the real-life romance that floated around me and for all of the magical fairy tales that graced my dreams, nothing would captivate my heart and soul the way Westley and Buttercup would in *The Princess Bride*. Up until age twelve, I had never watched a love story that wasn't animated, with animals singing and dancing across the screen. Not only that: I had never seen a love story that filled me with so much hope, desire, and adoration for this sentiment shared between two people.

As I sat through this movie, captivated as Westley fought evils and endured long-suffering separation to be reunited with his one true love, I discovered what I wanted most out of love. I realized then that it was the pursuit. I wanted to *be* Buttercup. I wanted no mountain to be too big, no battle to be too hard, no villain to be too daunting. I wanted to be a part of a love story that even death could not stop. I wanted to be the girl worth fighting for, the girl worth waiting for, the girl in which it took his all to obtain my love.

I wanted the pursuit.

That's where the lines continued in my little red notebook, and where the mental notes of what my own love story would look like poured out. Or rather, *whom* that love story would include. I believed with childlike faith that God, if I asked Him, would see my list and work as matchmaker to bring "that guy" to me. My perfect companion. My plus-one. My future husband. From my young heart to my giant God—in whom I believed nothing was impossible—I wrote out my wish list for my future husband. I titled it, "That Guy."

That guy would love me and pursue me to the ends of the earth.

That guy would be tall. (Because I was so tall, I wanted him to be taller.)

And dark. And handsome.

That guy would be playful.

That guy would love Jesus.

Oh how I longed for the pursuit, but after I wrote how I wanted "that guy" to love Jesus, it made me pause. I realized if I had the pursuit of a guy who did not love the Lord, the whole love story would be futile. I had to change the list. Ripping up the paper, I started over. I had to put *Relationship with God* first on the list. Number One, "that guy" would love Jesus. Everything else just ends up being toppings on an ice cream sundae. As the years went on, my young mind remained certain that God cared about all the desires of my heart, and so my list continued, sprinkles and all.

That guy would be a hard worker.

That guy would be kind and compassionate.

That guy would be funny and laugh at my jokes.

That guy would be from Texas or at least love the Dallas Cowboys!

That guy would be a good dancer.

That guy would break the speed limit.

And on and on my list went. Pages upon pages of the guy I knew would become my husband. Pages of the characteristics I loved about the marriages around me. Pages of qualities that were desirable just for me, and pages of a beautiful love story that would sweep me off my feet, defeating any enemy in its path.

As the years went by and I grew older, I would find myself coming back to this list many times to reflect and pray about "that guy." And as I would gaze over my bullet points of desires, I often found myself stopped by one specific line.

That guy would break the speed limit.

Why did I write that? Why was that important to me? It took some time, but I became aware that my longing was for a man who was not only handsome, God-fearing, and strong, but also a man who was imperfect. I knew if my whole list of amazing qualities came to life in a real human being, "that guy" would be flawless. Perfect. Too good. I knew that I wasn't perfect and that I could not measure up to a man who didn't make mistakes. I realized then that when my heart wrote out "would break the speed limit," it was telling me that any guy who broke the rules and made mistakes would also have enough grace in his heart for me to do the same.

He didn't need to be perfect.

I didn't need to be perfect.

We just needed to be perfect for each other.

Four
Imperfections

> You can't go to the ball looking like that!
> —*Cinderella*

I GUESS EVERY RELATIONSHIP HAS TO GO THROUGH IT AT SOME TIME. Any relationship that is worth having *needs* to go through it at some time.

It's never fun and it's seldom pretty. But, inevitably, it has to happen.

Every relationship needs to have its first fight. It's what softens up our sharp edges and clears away the cobwebs from our hearts. It's what brings us closer together and shows us our truest selves.

I was fourteen years old when it happened.

When I had my first fight with God.

It began the night I was getting ready for my first high school dance. An experience that was, for me, both terrifying and a delight all rolled into one.

Wanting this night to be perfect, I carefully put on makeup and curled my hair, taking hours to put myself together. When all of the prepping was said and done, I felt ready to put on my dress and head outside to take pictures. I was so proud of my bright turquoise-blue dress, and I knew that the color alone would make me stand out in the crowd, which is exactly what I wanted—that was, until I put it on.

As I looked in the mirror, rather than filled with joy at my appearance, I was horrified at the image staring back at me.

It was immediately obvious that the dress was too tight, and you could see every perceived imperfection of my body. My stupid big boobs, over which, coincidentally, I never wore anything tight because I had heard enough from boys who couldn't keep their comments to themselves. Plus, there were the rolls from my stomach and the side of my hips, which people affectionately call "love handles." Deep within my memory I could hear the lingering gasp of Cinderella's Fairy Godmother: "You can't go to the ball looking like that!"

I am fat, I thought.

I had to do something. I had to lose ten pounds in thirty minutes! I had to feel better about myself, to feel beautiful, to get back to how I felt before I put the dress on, desiring to be the center of attention for all of the reasons I deemed right.

It's the strangest thing, really, the way it suddenly occurs.

For years, there were details that went completely unnoticed, and then, in one moment, it's all I seemed to notice. As though a spotlight had been pointed directly at me, and all the subtleties that made up who I was suddenly felt like glaringly obvious imperfections.

Growing up, my dad would say that duct tape could fix anything, so I decided to put that statement to the test. Taking off my dress, I started from my hips—round and round I went with the tape, flattening all my rolls, inching my way up, covering up my imperfections strip by strip. And now, with my body covered in a sticky, gray, duct-tape suit, I slipped the dress on again, and *Boom!* It seemed as if my problem was solved. I made my own shaping undergarments before Spanx even existed!

Knowing fully that this haphazard version of a corset may have been ridiculous and may have made it difficult to breathe, I was still happy with the end result and was willing to forgo air to have the look I desired. My extra fat was sucked in and I was, again, for this moment in time, able to feel confident, ready to enjoy a night I was sure I would remember forever.

The theme of the dance was "The Jewel of the Nile," and despite the simplicity of the student council decorations—a hand-drawn sphynx from someone in art class, a couple colorful balloons hanging near the photo booth, and streamers draped around the gym walls—to me, it seemed perfect. I was here to meet up with my friends, looking like a jewel myself in my turquoise dress. I wanted this night to be one where I shone brightly, where I could enjoy every moment completely confident in the person that I was.

I remember feeling the reverberation of the loud music as a different picture of the gymnasium appeared each time the strobe lights would flash. All around me friends waved to one another, yelling over the beats of the music as they invited them into their group or complimented them on their look for the night. As I scanned the room, I ran into a friend of mine.

"Wow, Leanne, that dress makes you look so much skinnier than you really are!" she hollered over the music.

Instead of a smile, heat crept to my face as I received the first jolt of the night.

Was that a compliment, or was she saying I was fat? I thought.

In an effort to respond without creating awkwardness, I squeaked out, "Thanks!" quickly moving away from her and back into the crowd. While I tried to console myself from the hurt that I felt, in my heart I knew what she said was true: I wasn't skinny, this look tonight was just a façade, and I began to fear that people could see right through it.

Though her comment had thrown me for a bit of a loop, I quickly reunited with some of my closest friends, piling together at the photo booth. Being with them gave me such contentment, and the excited anticipation that I came to the dance with filled my heart again. The photographer instructed us to smile and say, "I like dancing!" as she snapped the picture. And, in what seemed to be an outpouring of my internal feelings, I put my smile on, loudly calling out the words, "I like dancin'!"

And then, in a blink, the second jolt hit me like a brewing storm.

"Did you hear Leanne? Aah lak dancin'!" Two boys, who were standing next to us waiting for their turn, snickered to each other just loud enough for all to hear.

It was as if someone had punched me in the gut, and all I could feel was my body tense in anger, my gaze falling to the floor as my heart sank in humiliation once again. At that moment, another one of my insecurities crept into my mind: my thick Texan accent. As much as I loved my mother, she had an accent thicker than the prize chili in a cook-off. Although I loved my mom dearly, I wasn't proud of my Texas twang, and unfortunately that trait was passed down to me. Why couldn't I have inherited the way she laughs instead?

I knew everyone heard those boys, and I wanted to crawl away and hide to get away from the awkwardness of this moment. But, determined not to let the boys best me, I forced myself to look up, gave a half-hearted grin, and pushed past them as if it weren't a thing.

While I left that scene with a bitter taste in my mouth, I was still determined to have a good night, to let it go, to move on, but at some point, something about this night started to feel like an attack. At first, it was the thoughtless comment made by a passing friend, then the boys, and soon, like a full-on Southern lightning storm, it seemed as though each and every one of my insecurities was being put on display for all to see.

The last thunderous jolt was from a couple of guys who eyed me and then made comments about me being too tall to dance with, adding that maybe it wouldn't be so bad because they would get to be eye-level with a large pair of knockers. Holding back tears, I backed away, finding a seat at a table, hoping that I could avoid any other personal attacks.

I came to this dance filled with excitement, but as the night marched on, the reality was that I was not experiencing the same fun as everyone else in the room seemed to be having. In fact, it became glaringly obvious that instead of enjoying myself, I was backing away from it all, cowering into the corner like a wallflower, avoiding anything that would pull me apart any further. And now these imperfections were all I could see.

My overweight figure.

My thick Texan accent.

My towering height.

My well-endowed chest.

I guess, looking back, this was the first time the devil really started to make himself known since the incident with the pictures on my wall. However, his appearance was more subtle and manipulative now. He crawled into my mind and took a stronghold by creating and preying on these insecurities. He convinced me that God had made a mistake and that He didn't really know what He was doing. Satan took the quiet little corners of my mind and began filling them with doubt.

And so the battle began. God and my faith on one side. The devil and his deceit on the other side. A very human fourteen-year-old body in the middle.

I began to take this lens of comparison that the devil had placed before me and allow it to take root, to cause tension, to create a struggle between the person that I was and the person I thought I needed to be. I used the way boys reacted to me as a measuring stick, a gauge of my worthiness, and soon the list of things I wanted to change began to grow, while the list of things I once loved about myself began to shrink into the background. I wanted to believe that I was beautifully and wonderfully made, but for some reason I wrestled to live in that space for much of my young life. And despite having a home that created space for me to grow in my faith and in my confidence, I still struggled with many of the parts of myself that God had given me. I thought that if I could just lose ten more pounds, change my hair, or adjust how I spoke, I would feel more whole, more complete, more loveable. And so, in an effort to find myself, I often began looking at other women around me in order to compare myself. And, as I dug deep into this comparison game, I could feel a tangible struggle growing between God and I, the struggle that began with that first fight.

I began to question Him and how He created me, wondering why I couldn't simply be more gentle, more peaceable, more feminine. And, as I grew in age, this battle of contentment in who God made me to be raged in my life, digging its roots deep into my bones, tangling itself so tightly only God could pull them out.

I just didn't know it at the time.

After the dance, I rushed into my room, pushed the golf bag from off the covers, and curled up on my bed, staring at the friendship bracelets that dangled from my vanity mirror. I was sure that God could have planned out something far less imperfect than this. And so we began to fight about it.

Or rather, I fought with Him and He listened.

> *God, why did I have to be like this?*
>
> *I don't understand what's wrong with me. Why would You create me to look like this?*
>
> *And not only that, but why did girls get stuck with all the bad parts? You made male bodies, and You made female bodies, but you gave too many hard things to the girls of this world. Why do we have to have breasts? And a period once a month? Which is gross and super embarrassing, by the way! And crazy emotions to go along with that period?*
>
> *Why did You make me loud and active if what You really wanted us girls to have was a gentle and quiet spirit?*
>
> *I'm mad and hurt because it feels like You don't see me, and I don't matter.*

After my heartfelt baring of my soul, I let the tears slide down the side of my face and onto my pillow.

Growing up in the church, I've heard many times that God speaks to us through the Bible to share His truth, to communicate His love, to give sight to the blind.

But He can also throw His own punches, making His points clear, and win in any fight with those words that come from the Good Book.

Then, grabbing my Bible for some kind of answer, I randomly opened up the pages to somewhere in the middle. And God, in His perfect understanding, began to ask His own questions directly from His Word: "Where were you when I laid the foundation of the earth? / Tell me, if you have understanding. / Who determined its measurements—surely you know!" (Job 38: 4–5, English Standard Version). As an exclamation point, the Lord God made His point clear: "Shall a faultfinder contend with the Almighty? / He who argues with God, let him answer it" (Job 40:1–2, ESV).

As I sat staring down at the pages, I knew I had no answer, and I was not God. Instead of being angry God had won this fight, I felt comforted that my God was higher, bigger, and far superior than my human mind. Since He created the world and since I couldn't create something out of nothing, I could surely trust that there were reasons that He created me the way I am. And so, knowing this, I laid my insecurities down at His feet.

I wanted to be seen. I wanted to matter. And it became clear to me that by following Him, trusting in Him, and allowing Him to take hold of my heart into His loving Hands, I would be the most beautiful version of myself imaginable. In surrendering to Him, I realized that the moment He formed me with His Hands in my mother's womb, I was already seen and I mattered.

However, when I took things back into my own hands, I forgot this. I looked in all the wrong places. I looked in broken mirrors, I reached for broken people, I sought a broken truth.

And ultimately it would leave me with a broken heart.

Five
Candy Hearts

> It's no use going back to yesterday,
> because I was a different person then.
>
> —*Alice's Adventures in Wonderland*[3]

I WAS A SOPHOMORE IN HIGH SCHOOL WHEN I SAW HIM FOR THE FIRST TIME. I was in the driver's seat of my Buick LeSabre, as my friends and I were getting ready to head out for pizza during our off-campus lunch hour. His name was Spencer, and he was leaving basketball practice with his friends for lunch. They walked past us, and, in the most casual way, he simply nodded his head and said, "Hi."

"You know, those freshman guys can't drive. We should totally offer to take them with us to the pizza place," my one friend suggested.

In a bold move of courage, we shouted out the windows for them to join us and made room in the car. As our fifteen- and sixteen-year-old bodies piled into the back and the space between all of us became smaller, a strange yet familiar tension began to fill the air.

It's seldom ever easy being a teenager. The changes, the growth, the hormones. But it's especially not easy being a Christian teenager growing up in the Bible Belt of North Texas.

---

3 *Alice's Adventures in Wonderland*, in *Alice's Adventures in Wonderland & Through the Looking-Glass*, with illustrations by John Tenniel (Hertfordshire, UK: Wordsworth's Classics, 1993), 102–03.

We faced the same struggles and pressures that any of our peers did, except that many of us had the added challenge of trying to navigate our way through a silent wilderness of adolescent curiosity. Adults never really discussed sex or lust or desire very much where we came from. They simply never talked about it, other than to say that it should be saved for marriage on all accounts. So we ended up hearing about it from movies and from our friends. Inaccurate testimonies at worst. Cautionary tales at best.

We heard whispers around the basketball courts and in the school halls about what could happen when left unsupervised, about the scandalous lines that could potentially be crossed. We weren't just encouraged to abstain from having sex, though; we were taught to withhold all physical affection until marriage, or at least that is what was etched into our minds. All the while, we weren't taught what to do with all of the feelings that surfaced in the meantime.

In a lot of ways, though, that is what this period in my life felt like: all or nothing. The pendulum of my conscience swung abruptly between purity or sin, good or bad, heaven or earth. Being a teenager felt completely consumed with making decisions, and none of them were somewhere in the middle. It didn't feel like there was room for more than one choice or to live somewhere in between. And so, as I wrestled with these feelings, I also wrestled in my relationship with God. Despite my love for Him, I also wanted to be seen, to be loved, to be known by boys. And for some reason, I couldn't find a middle ground. It was here or there, this or that, yes or no. And no one told me that it was God who created these desires in the first place. The desire for closeness with a boy. The desire for hand-holding and kissing. The desire to be known. The desire for more. No one told me that God actually designed me to want these things and that these desires were right and normal. And no one told me that God's design was also all about timing.

So we lingered. We floated around in a sort of adolescent purgatory, stuck between our natural desire to indulge our flesh and our spiritual desire to please our God. It wasn't an easy place to be, and either option left us feeling a tension that was often difficult to reconcile and even more difficult to resist.

Spencer and I were only friends at first. I remember him sitting in the back of my car, on our way to the pizza place, and thinking to myself that he was super cute and funny. As cute and funny as a freshman could be, I suppose. We laughed together and both enjoyed sports and attended youth groups, although at different churches. In some ways, our worlds naturally intertwined, and in other ways, we were from opposite sides of the tracks. He came from a difficult childhood and endured challenges that I never experienced in my own family life. He was independent and rough around the edges, but more because he had to be. Life had handed him a different set of cards, and he was playing them the best way he knew how. He wanted to belong to a different kind of life, and after my recent bouts of insecurities, I wanted to be seen through a different set of eyes. So it's not entirely surprising that we managed to find our way to each other.

Our relationship happened almost without us even noticing that it was evolving. We didn't realize the feelings that were brewing until they had already risen to the surface. Months were spent sharing more and more time together until a year had passed and we found ourselves on our first date.

"You know, since I went to homecoming with my friends, we never danced with each other," I said coyly to him after we went out for burgers.

Not one to miss a subtle hint, Spencer parked in front of my house and with the radio playing through the open car windows, we slow-danced in the driveway. No big event. No ornate flowers. No bright lights.

Just us. Doing life on our terms.

That first date was followed by about half a dozen more. But we were never officially a "couple." He would pursue a commitment from me, and I would reject the idea at the hands of superficial formalities. Comparing Spencer to that guy on my list,

He was too young.

He was too short. (He was taller than me, but only by an inch or two.)

He was too skinny.

He simply wasn't really my type.

Regardless of what my list said would be my perfect guy, a relationship began to happen. I don't think I intended it to, but somewhere, in between meeting that first day and ending up in his truck one evening, we became more than just friends.

Spencer was wearing his trademark polo shirt and a pair of jeans. I was wearing a plain black button-down shirt with short shorts to show off my long legs. We had spent hours in his old blue farm truck, "sucking face," as we like to put it. Desire to lock lips won, while the list of rules failed. And that's when I said it to him. That's when I spared him the agony of asking me a fourth time.

"Okay, Spencer ... I guess you can call me your girlfriend now."

He jumped, hollered, and pounded his hand on the cab of the truck. When his act of lunacy threatened to make me change my mind, he immediately stopped and promised to behave himself. And just like that, in our usual manner, we laughed. And I, Leanne, had a new man in my life.

Our time together was innocent bliss. Like most first loves, we got lost in the simple rhythm of our small-town life. We saw each other every day. During basketball season, we would hang out between practice and stay late to watch each other's games. After practice during my competitive golf season, we would sneak away, just the two of us, to play golf and kiss in between shots. Midweek, we would attend the First Baptist youth group or hang out at his grandparents' place to watch a television that had no more than three stations.

All in all, we were like any other high school couple. We got along, and when it came to my "that guy" list, he slowly started adding various shades of gray to my black-and-white ideas. For every one thing that he wasn't, he was something else that I didn't even know I wanted.

And lists can do that to us sometimes, if we're not careful. They can build barriers around the potential of what something *could* be by becoming so focused on what our list says something *should* be. So when Spencer and I set out to save Christmas one year, I came to realize that my list was about to be changed in ways I never expected.

In high school, I had a habit of compartmentalizing guys into various categories. We had the jocks, the gamers, and the band junkies—who liked to play music while getting lost in their dreams of being huge rock stars. And while all of these guys pursued different passions, they still seemed to have one thing in common: they all seemed to cuss like sailors. And by default, this eliminated them from any possibility of making my list. Maybe it was because my parents never cursed in our home. Maybe it's because hearing my dad yell out "Kiss a Pig!" when he was upset just left me full of giggles. Maybe it's because all of my parents' chosen expletives just sounded funny in comparison to any crude language.

Regardless, one of the items on my list was that I wanted a guy who didn't feel like he had to curse to be a man.

However, as Spencer and I spent more time together, he showed me that, when inserted appropriately, expletives could add a little spice to an otherwise dull point. So I began to learn the origin of certain curse words and come up with an alternative of my own. It was a quirk about myself that— even if no one else understood or appreciated—I still found incredibly funny. Having said that, it also wasn't a part of myself that I often shared with those around me.

But sometimes things happen.

Sometimes trees fall.

And sometimes the words just come out.

One Thanksgiving, as Spencer and I were spending time at his grandparent's house, we overheard his granny declare, "We just won't have a Christmas tree this year!" Apparently, the fake tree they had put up for years had given its last performance by breaking a leg, taking it from center stage to garbage can. Shocked and appalled, we took it upon ourselves to find the perfect tree, cut it down, and, in turn, bring Christmas back to its rightful place in his grandmother's home.

We marched into the woods like the lumberjacks we thought ourselves to be, with hatchets in hand and one goal in mind. The temperature had dropped, and it was beginning to feel a lot like Christmas. We ended up finding what we thought to be a beautiful nine-foot-tall pine tree, which turned out to be more like a six-foot-tall juniper shrub. No matter! Regardless of its appearance, it would most certainly suffice. So, as Spencer would say, "We hacked the crap out of that tree," put it in the back of his truck, and brought it to the house, pine needles and all.

Once we got home, we spent hours decorating our plunder

with ornaments and wrapping it in tinsel. When it came time for the final touch—the magical star—Spencer stood on the edge of the couch, carefully reached across the tree, and just at the same moment, the tree began to fall ... on me! Now, this tree may not have seemed overly daunting at first glance, but when its branches reached out to hug me at all angles, I knew that a set of carefully curated words were about to spill out of me. So as the tree made its final lunge toward me, panicking, I screamed out, "DOO-DOO BALLS!" and hit the ground, with Christmas ornaments falling and rolling and shattering around me. Spencer, completely thrown off guard by my choice of language, let the tree go and watched as it landed on top of me. Then, like saving a drowning person from the waves, Spencer grabbed my arms, pulled me out, as we sat laughing and looking at our sideways Christmas tree. However, knowing all things can be fixed with duct tape, we proceeded to use my favorite tool to secure the tree to the wall and, for the second time that day, saved Christmas!

However, like any true mission, a debrief was required, and in this one, Spencer needed to know ...

"What the heck is doo-doo balls?"

I then went on to explain that *doo-doo balls* was just another name for crap. Only it's worse because *doo-doo balls* means you are constipated, and constipation is worse than just plain crap. "It's my own personal cuss word."

I stared at him, with anticipation, waiting to see what this new layer of myself would reveal in him. He looked at me, as the corners of his mouth slowly started to curl up into the most endearing smile, and enthusiastically declared, "That's so ridiculously weird that it makes sense!" and we doubled over in laughter together. The kind of laugh that washed away any insecurity I may have had. The kind of laugh that wraps you up in its arms and reminds you that you are loved.

From that moment on, if we ever forgot our homework or stubbed a toe or missed a putt at mini golf, we knew exactly what to say. And every time we did, we shared that same body-shaking, deep-in-your-gut belly laugh. A laugh that no one understood but us. A laugh that always brought me back to that moment.

It was a moment that helped me to understand that there was more to a guy—and to love—than what I *thought* I wanted.

Being with Spencer was contentment at its finest. It was fun. It was comfortable. It was natural. All things I soon added to my list.

In a lot of ways, our time together was spent the same way as our time spent apart, except with each other by our side. Now the more basic parts of our day were spent with jokes and more laughter. We were happy, and it never occurred to us that one day we wouldn't be. Our relationship wasn't marked by our initials being carved in a tree or matching bracelets that we each wore. Instead, we were marked by a strange void that resided deep within each of our hearts, and, somehow, holding hands made the hole feel smaller.

I wanted to feel desired, and he adored every breath that I took. Like the puppy he once gave me as a gift, he followed my every move and longed to be with me at every moment. He wanted to feel stability, and I took him as mine, buying him lunch when he didn't have the money and teaching him golf when he had never played. I looked upon him and his choices as something to be guided and his life as something to be steered. Together, we served a purpose: to make the other feel more whole. And on Valentine's Day that same school year, we said the words that we had never shared before with anyone other than family. Surrounded by stuffed animals and chocolate candies and cut-out hearts, we exchanged glances as I read the card he had handed to me ...

"I know it's really soon, and I'm not supposed to say this, but it's how I feel, so I'm just going to say it anyway ... I love you."

My heart skipped a beat, and though I felt the same way, I was scared to say it out loud. So instead, I grabbed the pink box of candy hearts sitting next to me and, looking through each message, found the one with "I love you" stamped on the front and handed it to him. Cheesy, I know, but that's what it was. And from then on, that's who we were: two young people in love. And the thing about falling in love is that it becomes a part of you. It can never be undone. For all the rest of your days, you have given a piece of yourself to another human being. Your heart alters. Your soul expands. Your being changes. And regardless of what happens from that point on—be it young love or great love or true love—we are shaped by those with whom we share those words.

So this is why it came like a bombshell when, the next school year, right before homecoming of my senior year, we were sitting in his truck again—the same truck where we first decided to be a couple—and he told me that he wanted to stop dating me.

He wanted to *stop* dating me.

The boy that had persistently asked me to be his girlfriend, the boy who worshipped the ground I walked on, wanted to break up with me. Not because he didn't like me anymore. Not because he didn't love me anymore. Not because he didn't want to spend time with me anymore. But because, suddenly, he had been noticed. The "young underclassman" I had always known was now growing into his muscles and his height and a new sense of self. He realized that now, when he would walk down the hall, the once-blank stares from those around him shifted to admiring glances, coy smiles, and flirtatious words. He was curious about more than just me now. He wanted to explore his options.

And it destroyed me.

I could feel it in my body as the words left his mouth. I could feel my chest tightening and my stomach turning and my heart racing. My mind filled with thoughts of doubt and insecurity. The same insecurities that had already plagued me suddenly felt magnified alongside a hundred new ones.

Was I too chunky?

Was I not appealing?

Was my accent too brash?

Was I too tall?

Was I good enough at anything?

I left his truck that day and walked through the front door of my house. And, dropping my bags at the door, I marched down the hall and slammed my bedroom door behind me. As the air left my lungs in a giant exhale of desperation, I fell onto my bed. Arms wide, face down, spread eagle. I fell.

I fell into sadness.

I fell into grief.

I fell into despair.

And when the time came for me to finally rise again, it would be as a completely different person.

Six

The Exchange

All alone, my pet? ... Go on, have a bite.
—*Snow White and the Seven Dwarfs*[4]

He either will or he won't.
It's worth a shot.
I'm 100 percent sure it's a maybe.

It had been four weeks since Spencer had ended our relationship, and I was anxious for him to see me, the new me. During this time, I had lost a few pounds, gained a new hairstyle, and believed that some of the imperfections I had—the reasons he may have broken up with me—were changed. There was a basketball game that night, and I knew that he would be there, so I left my house in eager anticipation, wanting to win back the boy I couldn't stop thinking about, the boy who consumed my mind, the boy who I desired with every fiber of my being.

As I entered the gym, my heart full of uneasy hope, I looked around, waiting to catch his eye. The room was packed, music was blaring in the background, the sounds of the basketballs dribbling reverberated off of the walls, and the laughter of friends rang loudly in the stands.

Keep your emotions pulled together and avoid any situation that might cause you to look foolish, I thought. Because I wanted

---

4   *Snow White and the Seven Dwarfs* (Burbank, CA: Walt Disney Productions, 1937), directed by William Cottrell, David Hand, et al, 123 min.

him to want me again, and that meant I had to do whatever it took to keep him from seeing how I was really feeling on the inside, which was uncertain, anxious, and cautiously optimistic. And I thought that for this brief time, this one basketball game, this first encounter since the breakup, he would see me and want to be with me again.

Glancing around the gym, my heart pounding out of my chest, I continued to keep my eye out for Spencer. And then I saw him. Not alone, but with another girl. A smiling, skinny, beautiful girl, and she had his full attention.

And as I stood among this same crowd of people, everything went silent. The tiny bit of hope that clung to my spirit, the part of me that dreamt of this moment, the moment when I imagined he would fall back in love with me, just broke. Suddenly I couldn't hear, I couldn't see straight, I couldn't breathe. I felt paralyzed as those broken bits of hope started to crumble beneath my feet; I felt like I wanted to die. Soon my entire body began to tense as bile rose from my stomach up into my throat, taking every ounce of strength to keep my insides from spilling out. It felt like I was in the teacup ride at the state fair, spinning around and around. I wanted to get out of there. I wanted to cry. I wanted to scream. But I couldn't. I was determined to not let him see me fall apart.

Instead, I walked in.

I sat down.

I faked a smile. And I kept my stomach from betraying me for nearly half the game. For now, for these few quarters I had to look strong, but I just wasn't ready for this. I wasn't ready to see him laughing with another girl, smiling at her, looking at her with the admiration he once had for me. I wasn't ready to be confronted with the reality that our relationship was over. The reality that he was with someone new and had seemed to have all but forgotten me.

And quickly I could feel myself losing control of my emotions. Each passing minute, reminding me of my heartbreak all over again. Every passing second, inching me closer to my bursting point.

And so, with what little strength I had remaining, I left the scene of my heart's fatality. I hopped in my gray Buick LaSabre, making my way home and back to my room, crying until the pain turned to anger. Crying until there were no more tears left to fall. Crying until I had resolved something in my heart. I decided at this moment that I wasn't going to feel this way anymore and I would find a way to get him back.

No one tells you what to do after a relationship falls apart. No one tells you how to navigate those first feelings of loss, rejection, and emptiness. To be honest, I don't think anyone really knows what to say when you have experienced a blow that shakes you to your core, causing the reality you know and the comfort that you love to be demolished. No one tells you how to walk through pain that raw, that vulnerable, that crushing. Instead, you are told only that you will make it to the other side, that you *have* to make it to the other side. And because of this, the end of love—especially of a first love—can become an excruciatingly lonely place to be.

The months after Spencer and I broke up were some of the hardest days I can remember. Not only was I as an eighteen-year-old girl struggling to keep myself together emotionally on a day-to-day basis at school, but I also felt isolated from those around me. I had often chosen time with Spencer over time with my friends and, in turn, space had grown between my girlfriends and me. And because of that, I felt embarrassed crawling back to them. I didn't know how to reconnect, and so I chose to remain disconnected. To keep to myself. To walk through this season without them.

I also put my parents at arm's length. Looking back, I can see how my parents, especially my mom, struggled during this time. Though they believed that the ending of this relationship was the best thing for me, they also struggled to see me in so much pain. I spent many nights alone, hiding out in the shower, believing that the rush of water would cover the sounds of my cries. And I remember my mom sharing with me how she stood outside the bathroom door, hearing those cries I had hoped were inaudible. I remember her sharing how much it hurt her to hear me, knowing that there was nothing she could do to take this feeling away from me. She did her best to cheer me up, to take me shopping or out to eat. She tried to busy my mind and help me to move forward, hoping that these distractions would show me glimmers of joy amid my despair.

My friends and family weren't the only ones being forced to cope with the fallout of my broken heart. Eventually, I found myself quarrelling with God about the pain I was enduring. I remember sharing with Him, crying out to Him about how I believed our relationship was good, that I believed it was right, and that I even thought that Spencer might be my husband someday. I remember crying out that I didn't understand why I had to experience this grief, that I didn't want to experience this loss, that I didn't want to live like this. I knew that I trusted the Lord, but I also realized in my heart that if this was the road I was going to have to walk down, then He and I were going to hit a roadblock. I wanted to do what was right in His eyes, but I also wanted to experience peace again, to experience love again, to experience happiness again, and I was willing to take that pursuit into my own hands if necessary.

Because I was shutting anyone out who could help me

work through the turbulent emotions I had been feeling, my body began to reveal on the outside the turmoil I was feeling on the inside. It became a physical representation of what was going on deep inside my heart. Over the course of about two months, I had lost fifteen pounds. I couldn't eat. I couldn't sleep. I couldn't think. My body now revealed how broken I felt, how shattered I became, how desperate I was to put all of the broken parts of myself back together again. In many ways, the ending of our relationship left me in pieces; the parts of myself that I identified with, that made me who I was, were stripped away, leaving me feeling exposed in ways that I hadn't experienced since the run of shame down my parent's driveway. I may not have been standing outside with my clothes in a pile at my feet, but emotionally I felt naked, vulnerable, afraid.

It was a season of agony.

Of loneliness.

Of hopelessness.

Of brokenness.

Of devastation.

And this is right where Satan wanted me. I felt utterly alone, and by choosing to sit in that loneliness, I became a danger to myself. I had distanced myself from the friends and family who could offer me comfort, support, and wisdom to navigate through this season of life, and this distance caused my mind to become clouded, leading me to impulsively choose what I thought was best for myself. And so, like Snow White in the absence of her seven wise companions, I took a bite of the poison apple set before me and I fell.

Into temptation.

Into desire.

And, ultimately, into bed.

It had been just two months after seeing Spencer at the basketball game when holiday season arrived. A time when everyone is celebrating and hearts are supposed to be filled with joy and love and peace. A time when we hold our loved ones close and cherish the time and memories that we have with them. But this holiday, instead of feeling joy, contentment, and peace, I felt desperation. I wanted to return to the happy times, the times filled with laughter, with hiking in the woods, with inside jokes. But now I carried those memories by myself; I just had doo-doo balls by myself. And it felt like shit.

I was so desperate for the relationship between Spencer and I to rekindle itself, and I hated myself for feeling that way. I hated that I felt so tied to him, but I didn't know how to set myself free. I wanted him back, and I had resolved in my heart that I would do whatever it took to have him again: his attention, his affection, his adoration.

It was just before Christmas that the opportunity presented itself. Spencer's mother had invited me over to visit during the holiday. She and I had talked a few times during the breakup, and she had said that Spencer had to work late this particular evening and that I was welcome to come over to spend a little time with her catching up. It was hard enough processing through the breakup with Spencer, but what I didn't expect was the grieving that came when I had to simultaneously sever ties with the friends and family that came along with our relationship. I adored all of Spencer's family, and it was equally as hard to not see them in this breakup, so I was excited to spend some time with her. As I sat in the living room talking with Spencer's mom, I heard the door open and watched him walk through the front door. Spencer got off work early, and the two of us found ourselves together again in familiar territory, though this time under very different terms. Seeing each other from across the room caused a rush of emotions to run through me, causing my heart to race and my body to shake. The intensity of these emotions quickly took my breath away, and all I could think about was how I wanted to be close to him again. Up until this point, Spencer and my relationship was what I considered to be innocent in nature. Starry-eyed, intense kissing, fondling caresses. No more, no less. Truthfully, it wasn't up until this point that I believed our relationship needed more in order to keep us together. But it happened. Sometime during that visit, I realized it; I understood what I could offer in exchange to free myself from this pain. I realized that this relationship, if it were going to be rekindled, was going to need some lighter fluid, something to ignite that spark and bring it back to life quickly. And I believed that if I pursued him, if I offered him my body, fully and completely, this hurt that was digging deeper and deeper in my heart would be replaced with peace. That I would feel wanted. That I would feel desired. That I would feel worthy and whole again.

After a few weeks of talking on the phone, I did it. I found myself in my car on my way to Spencer's place, thinking about him, about us, and about what to do next. I knew I wanted him to be mine, and so I pulled into his driveway, walking away from the beautiful light of the day and into the darkness of his house, into his room, and into his bed. I pursued him. I was bold. I was seductive, and he was more than willing. And consciously, I handed over my body for his affection.

I bit the apple.

And its spell was cast.

I left his house alone, walking down the driveway to my car, my skin feeling oddly uncomfortable on my body. My pain had been taken away. But not in the way that I thought it would be. Emptiness had taken its place. I left his house that day with a deep feeling of regret. I was a virgin. And now I'm not. As I drove away, this gnawing feeling inside of me that I had just done something that I could never take back ate away at my bones. I walked into that house hoping to bring something back to life with my choice, but instead I just created something new, not something built on love or respect or adoration. But something motivated by fear, power, and control. Something that, eventually, became a black hole of shame, sadness, and a whole new kind of desperation.

Walking out of his house that day was a beginning. From that moment forth, we became two people who replaced our emotions with physical desire. We chased away the dark shadows in the room by satisfying our feelings of need and temptation. We craved each other like a drug, all the while knowing how toxic it was becoming. Every time I walked out my front door to see him, I heard God's voice urging me not to go. And every time I heard that voice, I shut the door behind me and continued on, believing that I knew better than God how to take the pain away.

It didn't take long before I couldn't recognize the person that I was becoming. Instead of running to God for comfort, I would sneak over to Spencer's house to feel desired, wanted, and seen. I knew that the peace I had been searching for wasn't being found in my relationship with Spencer, but for some reason I couldn't let it go. I couldn't let him go. And so I fell. Deeper and deeper, I fell into his arms, into my self-indulgence, into my sin.

The truth was that while I was living in my own skin, all the while I wanted to physically shed this person I had become. However, every time I tried with my own strength,

I was left trapped, suffocating in the snakelike skin I had grown for myself. I was a mess, I was lost, and what I really needed in order to escape was a change from the inside.

But you know what? Despite all of my mess and all of my self-inflicted brokenness, someone was still waiting for me.

He was lovingly listening when I had questions about who I was, about what I was doing, about the choices I had made.

He still saw me as a beautiful person created in His image, someone worth pursuing, and someone worth waiting for.

As I continued to live in brokenness for months and I questioned many of my decisions, I came to a point where I couldn't avoid Him any longer. His still, small voice became the only one worth listening to. Just as I longed for Spencer, for those feelings of comfort and feelings of security, I now longed to spend time with God again. To hear His words. To feel His forgiveness. To be guided by His gentle hand.

And, in the most unexpected of places, with a love like no other, He was there with the peace I had been searching for all along.

Seven
Crying Out

If you'd lost all your faith, I couldn't
be here. And here I am!

—*Cinderella*

THE SUMMER BEFORE MOVING AWAY TO COLLEGE, I remember walking outside of my parent's home on an early July morning to have one of the most important conversations of my life. As my Keds pounded the concrete driveway, I could feel the early morning humidity climb my legs.

Spencer and I had been in the throes of a purely physical relationship that began shortly after Christmas, when all the broken pieces of our young selves found comfort in our intimacy. But since that moment, when I walked out of his home and away from the scene of our temptation, the "we" that I used to know felt like it had died.

It also seemed as though the closer Spencer and I physically became, the further apart God and I became. I deeply struggled with the shame I felt about the choices I was making, and so I chose to put God at arm's length, ultimately creating a deep hole in my heart. It was like reliving heartbreak all over again, and I just wanted God back in my life.

And so I grabbed a skateboard leaning against the wall of the garage, walked out to the driveway, planted myself on it, and began an honest conversation with the Lord. One which I had been avoiding for quite some time.

Before any others could find their way out, the words

"Lord, it's me and I am sorry" blurted from my lips and, in so doing, opened up the floodgates, releasing both my tears and my heart before my Savior. For the first time, I verbally confessed my part in the destructive life I was living. I admitted that I had been willing to offer whatever was necessary to get Spencer back, and I acknowledged the price I had paid left me with a debt that only forgiveness could pay off. I shared with Jesus that all I wanted was to stop the hurt that filled my soul at having lost Spencer's love and attention, but instead, my actions had only caused a different kind of loss and pain. I apologized for desperately pursuing *my* way and completely disregarding His way. But I knew God was loving. And I knew God was good. And I knew God was forgiving. So I just kept on talking.

And like all good fathers, He listened, He loved, He wrapped His arms around me, and He made me feel whole again. Almost immediately I felt the ease and relief of His undying love flow through every part of my body, and I knew that I could be restored and find my way again. I knew I could beat the darkness that I had created. It was one of the most deeply profound realizations of my young life.

The next morning, I chose to break things off with Spencer. I told him that I wanted to cut ties, that I hated the person I had become, a person whose relationship is based solely on a physical connection, and that I wanted to focus on my relationship with the Lord. I knew that this was the perfect time for us to part ways, because I was leaving for college and we could both have a fresh start. And just like that, I ended the relationship I had tried so hard to rekindle. I walked away from the very thing I had sought after to take away my pain. He stood in the doorway of his house, looking unsure of what just happened, while I took a deep breath and walked away.

I had done it. I had conquered the enemy. I had defeated the monster I had created for myself.

Or so I thought.

I've heard it said that home isn't a place; it's a feeling. A month after breaking up with Spencer, I left the only home I had ever known in pursuit of a new one, the town of Lubbock, 218 miles West of Graham, where I had earned myself a golf scholarship to attend Texas Tech University.

Golf was always a part of my life, and since my dad was the golf coach in Graham, I was out at the course for hours on end whether I wanted to be there or not. While I did enjoy being in the company of my father, I didn't necessarily love the sport. However, over time, golf and I grew on each other. More practice led to better shots, and better shots led to a few trophies. It wasn't much of a surprise, then, that my parents encouraged me to go after a golf scholarship to pay for my college education. After all the hours I put in to determinedly overcoming the difficulties that dyslexia brought, my parents didn't want the opportunity for higher education to pass me by.

So during my senior year of high school, I put myself out there, sending my resume and videos to countless universities across the country. I wanted this so badly and was therefore certain to leave no stone unturned. While I didn't hear back from many, a few schools, including the University of Texas Tech, reached out to me for a visit. Luckily for me, this coach was interested in honing my skills instead of expecting a scratch golfer right off the bat, and ultimately he ended up throwing me a bone, offering me a 75 percent golf scholarship.

I longed so deeply to get out of Graham and prayed for a way to find escape from the bondage of my relationship with Spencer and all of the problems that it created. And so while some said that consistency led to this scholarship, I truly believed that this miracle was a direct answer to my prayer. With a heart full of excitement at this new adventure, I packed my bags and traveled west to Lubbock, Texas. A new address. A new home. A new beginning.

The transition of leaving home when you are eighteen years old is one of growing up and finding your place in the world. It is the gap between childhood and adulthood, the place where we start to become our own person. I was excited to break free from my small town and find out who I was and where I fit.

Settling into Lubbock came with the expectation that I would make new friends and attend a new church and begin a bright, beautiful new future. Instead, the complete opposite happened.

While being a student athlete at a major university had its perks, this "privilege" did come with a real segregation that I found set me up for isolation. We had our own dorm rooms, a workout gym, and a cafeteria. When I wasn't in class or at the course, I could likely be found in one of three places, most often my room. Due to a busy schedule and the stress of being in a new place all alone, I didn't branch out to socialize and therefore my single-person dorm room became a fortress of solitude. And so my days dragged on, going to on-campus classes, walking by nameless faces, and then heading to the golf course, playing with girls I never saw off of the green fairways.

The truth was that I found myself feeling secluded and distant most of the time. Meeting people was more difficult than I anticipated, and I felt equally disconnected from those I had left behind. I didn't belong in Graham anymore. But

I didn't belong in Lubbock either. I was homesick for a place that didn't exist.

Rainy days were the worst. When golf practice was cancelled and I had finished all my homework: that was when I really felt the depth of my solitude. Here I was, a girl, a bed, and a desk in a dorm room with nothing to do. These were the moments that sadness sat heaviest on my heart. I felt the vacant space. I felt the void. I felt the emptiness. I had no friends to call in Lubbock because I hadn't made any.

This season in my life, however painful, also opened the door for a renewed relationship with my mom. When I didn't have anyone else to call, I called her. I knew that I could cry on the phone with my mom and share with her how depressed and confused I felt about college life. I often told her that I felt lied to, that these were supposed to be some of the most exciting and fun years of my life, but instead all I felt was frustration, isolation, and loneliness. She was an ear to listen and always had a heart filled with love and compassion as I expressed my misfortune.

And when I couldn't stand to be in my dorm room anymore, I would wander through the walkways of campus or through the aisles of Walmart. I wandered just to do something—anything—to remove myself from the despair I felt.

Honestly, I just longed to feel seen again. And when all of these feelings became too much, I began to reach for that old familiar connection, that old comfort lying next to me, that Band-Aid to cover up my gaping wound. I reached out again to Spencer in hopes of making it all go away.

One phone call.

One three-and-a-half-hour drive back to Graham.

One lie from the Deceiver to push me to do things I would not have done before.

I had always done a good job of covering myself up and felt more comfortable that way—hiding my figure from the gawking eyes of boys. But now I wanted to get a certain boy's eyes to look. And as I pulled on the black lace top—showing off the very abundant cleavage that I used to curse in high school—I felt a mixture of emotions. Looking at myself in the mirror, I was confident I would get Spencer's attention especially since I gave parts of myself away so freely before, but I also felt incredibly awkward at the same time. Exposed. And now I was going to walk out in public. I was willing to do all of this so I didn't have to feel lost. So I didn't have to feel the loneliness. So I didn't have to wander around Walmart anymore. And as I slipped into bed next to the guy who felt a million miles away, I could also feel that old familiar gnawing as self-loathing began to eat away at my heart and soul again. And the only semblance of comfort I could find was in my weekly car ride.

Three and a half hours.

Three and a half hours alone in the quiet of my car.

Three and a half hours in the middle—not being here and not being there.

The landscape would pass by me with such stillness, and the road ahead would get lost in the horizon. The driver-side window would be open, and I would rest my left elbow on the edge of the doorframe as the warm Texas air would blow through my hair.

I made this drive every single weekend from Texas Tech back home to Graham. Three and a half hours spent somewhere in that place, that in-between place that gave me a few hours of peace. It was in this place that I didn't have to think about the turmoil I endured at home or the loneliness that crippled me at college. I always looked forward to this time on the road, where I could escape from my pain and the mess I had made. What I realized, however, was that these three and a half hours were not enough. Those nagging feelings would creep back in as the car would slow and my destination was within sight. I could feel my adversary inching closer, ready to pull me back into the cycle I was running from. And as I shut the ignition off and lifted my eyes to look at the horizon before me, I saw that the enemy I was running from, the enemy I thought I was outsmarting for those three and a half hours, wasn't hiding in a closet in my dorm room or lurking around a dark corner waiting to attack. Instead, I uncovered that the villain of my story was simply the person I saw staring back at me in the mirror.

Even at nineteen, I knew that this wasn't the person that I wanted to be. And though I couldn't necessarily articulate who it was I wanted to become, I still knew that my current existence wasn't it. I didn't want to be the girl who slept with some guy to avoid her pain. I didn't want to be the girl who disregarded God's voice to pursue her own pleasure. I didn't want to be the girl that lied in order to cover it all up. But that's what I was doing. And once I realized what I was capable of, I did what I needed to in order to keep what I wanted. Soon I began to pile sin on top of sin. And just like the pink sponge roller I tried to bury in the trash when I was ten, I tried to cover my physical sin with a pile of lies. I lied to my parents about Spencer. I lied about sex. I lied about who I was with and where I was going. It seemed to me, at this time in my life, that I lied to everyone and I lied about most everything. And with those lies, I also began to withdraw from any of the voices that were not in line with my own. I lied to save face. I lied to look pure. I lied so I could pretend that I wasn't doing the exact thing I had committed to leaving behind. And, in so doing, the surges of guilt over what I *was* doing began to numb. I wanted both—the comfort of a relationship with Spencer and the grace of a relationship with God—but I knew what He would say if I talked to Him. And, honestly, I didn't want to hear it.

So I turned my back. I pushed Him out of the picture. I avoided His nudges. I shut my ears to His gentle whispers. I looked the other way when He tried to redirect my gaze. But I think that something happens when we finally lose sight of ourselves, when we no longer recognize the person staring back at us in the mirror; we go back to someone who does. And that's what I did. Time and time again. Time and time again I cried out to God for forgiveness, for strength, for change, and time and time again he listened, he loved, and he gave me another chance.

I read once that "Your mercies are new every morning," and just as the sun would rise and set, so would my resolve to break free of my frailty. I would fall and always turn to God to help me up. I would fail and always ask for a way out. I would sin and always beg for redemption. And I clung to those mornings with sweet desperation.

In the morning I'm never going to fall again.

In the morning I'm never going to backslide.

In the morning I'm set on faithful obedience.

And then the night comes. And I am my own worst nightmare.

The sun went down, and I was once again a slave to my sin, a slave to my own personal comfort, and because of that bondage, each "sorry," each tear, each plea that I raised up to God didn't break a single chain. Instead, I was still holding myself back from the person He had destined me to be.

I still wanted a true love story.

I still longed for "That Guy."

I still hoped for a relationship built on truth and beauty. I desired a love so much more than I felt I deserved, but I was stuck. I had returned to living two lives: the life I wanted people to see, and the life that I was hiding from the world. I stayed in this in-between with Spencer for years, oftentimes not knowing where our relationship stood, but always aware that this was exactly where I did not want to be. I hated how I felt every time I hopped into the car to drive myself back home. I hated that I was using him to feel comforted, desired, and seen, despite my knowing that he was not that guy for me. And so, round and round we went, living in ambiguity, sin, and shame until God, in His perfect way, prepared another escape route just for me in the most unlikely of places—a summer golf conference.

The summer after I finished my freshman year of college, I attended a College Golf Fellowship Conference where I first heard the words of the lead pastor of a Bible church in Denton, Texas, and once again, God gave me hope. His teaching was about the Song of Solomon, and he discussed the topics of dating, marriage, and sex, the exact subject that was eating away at my heart, mind, and soul. As I listened, I began to fall in love with the story of Solomon, a man who follows after the Lord and pours out his life to love and care for his wife. But while I clung to every word about this man, I also realized that the characteristics of the bride in this Bible story were far from the girl I had turned out to be. However, I knew that the God of the Bible loves a good story of redemption, so I knew there was still hope for me. And soon I could feel this deep stirring inside of me. This new whisper. It was through this man's words about relationships and godly marriages that God turned my eyes toward Him once more, giving me a desire for a life made new. Again I could feel a new direction being placed before the compass of my life. And again, it was there that God had been patiently waiting, arms outstretched to embrace me and walk with me once more.

I truly believed that in order to experience the life God had planned for me, I needed to get out of Lubbock, and I needed to get away from my old patterns of rebellion.

My golf coach had once told me that what we focus our minds on often becomes our realities. He explained this to me one day as I was staring out at hole 6, an especially difficult par 3 with a huge water hazard spanning the distance between the green and me.

"What are you thinking about right now, Leanne?" he asked.

The answer was obvious to me: "Don't hit the ball in the water!"

"Well," he said, "most of the time, if you focus your energy on just avoiding the water, you will, in fact, hit the ball into the water—the very opposite of your intended goal. So you have to use what's known as replacement theory. It's simple but requires focused attention. Instead of focusing on the water, you have to focus on the green—your goal, your hope, your intended target. If you do this, if you focus your energy on where you want to be instead of where you don't want to go, you are much more likely to reach your goal."

This theory, this mindset was exactly what I needed. I realized that if I was going to follow God's plan for my life, there was going to have to be a change. And so I prayed for that replacement in my head and in my heart.

However, I didn't know it was going to take the biggest scare of my life to fix my eyes on Him.

It had been one week since I was supposed to get my

period. And as the days ticked by with no sign, that anxiousness quickly turned to worry.

On day fourteen, after two weeks of panic, I finally decided that I had to make that dreaded call. I had to make an appointment. I had to see if my worst fear was now my reality.

"Hello, uh yes, I uh need to make an appointment?" I squeaked, trying to hold my tears back.

"Yes, dear, and why is it that you need to see the doctor?" questioned the nurse.

"I, uhhh, I'm two weeks late!" I blubbered desperately.

After making the appointment, I quickly hung up the phone, collapsing to the ground and praying like a person on death row. Fear consumed every part of me, and all I could think of was to lay on the floor of my dorm room face down, arms spread wide, and cry out to the only one I knew would listen.

My God, my Father, my Savior,

Oh Lord, I need some saving! What have I done? What am I going to do now?

Stupid, stupid girl!

Jesus, I beg of You, please don't let me be pregnant! I'm broken apart. I'm at the end of my rope. I've dug the pit, and I'm sitting in it. How do I get out now?

Please, Jesus, save me from myself. I have to get out of this cycle. Lord, I'm tired of trying to run away from Spencer. I am tired of trying to run away from my problems. I have to run toward You. I need the replacement theory. I need to get to the place where I can learn my Bible, go to church, get a support system around me. Replace the "I don't want to see Spencer" with "I want to know and love Jesus." I have to get to that Bible church in Delton.

Oh Lord, I believe You are big enough. Please don't let me be pregnant, but at this point … even if I am, I have to get to Denton.

Getting there seemed impossible. But as I sat in the uncertainty of crippling fear with a longing for a new, restored life, God's hand was on me once again. It turned out that I was not pregnant, and, while terrifying, this test truly brought me to the end of myself. I knew now that I truly wanted Jesus and not a quick-fix relationship. My motivation had changed from that of running away to running toward Him. The truth was that He had been waiting for me all along. He was waiting so that He could make a way, so that He could open the doors I needed to rest in Him, and He did so by bringing one of my greatest encouragers to the forefront: my mom.

While I didn't tell her about my pregnancy scare, I did share with her my desire to get out of Lubbock, to move to Denton, and all of the anxieties that I had regarding the mountains that needed to move in order for me to get there. I shared about the impossible task that seemed to lie ahead. And while I poured my heart out to her, she waited for the opportunity to share a simple, yet powerful suggestion: to keep on praying. She knew that God could move all mountains and confirmed in my heart that all I had to do was ask. And so, with a pen in my hand, and my new, emerald-color journal on my lap, I wrote a list of prayers, placing each one like dreams in a hope chest, watching and waiting to see what would happen next.

Eight
God's Hand

> That in the ages to come He might show
> the exceeding riches of His grace.
>
> —*Eph. 2:7 (New King James Version)*

THE LIGHT POURED IN THE WINDOW ACROSS FROM ME. Bright beams of sun fell against the walls with such peace and solitude. Tiny flecks of dust floated in the room as though they were dancing to their own beat. It was a beautiful calm in the midst of turmoil. I wanted desperately to be delivered from my distress and the continual loneliness that overwhelmed me, and I knew there was only one way that I was getting out of Lubbock. And that was by God's hand.

As I sat in this light, I looked over the prayers that God needed to answer, all of the moves that God had to orchestrate in order for me to get away from this place and to Denton for the coming fall semester, and waited with faith enough to make it rain.

• • •

Lord, I need a 75 percent scholarship in order to transfer schools, but I don't even know where to begin.

While I had my heart set on leaving Texas Tech, I also knew that one of the significant hurdles I would need to jump was a monetary one. The only reason I had been able to attend college in the first place was through the blessing of a golf scholarship, the one that, according to NCAA regulations, I would forfeit if

I made any type of communication with another coach. Knowing that I couldn't reach out to the University of North Texas golf coach in Denton about a transfer filled me with uncertainty about how I would ever get out of Lubbock.

While I sat in frustration for some time over this seemingly insurmountable obstacle, my mom took matters into her own hands, immediately calling up Coach Kline, the head golf coach at UNT, to see what we could learn about scholarships and potential transfer opportunities.

The good old directness and determination from my mom was matched on the other end of the phone, as the coach was not interested in getting a transfer student. Not only that, Coach Kline had never given out a golf scholarship to anyone who wasn't a freshman, but she would be willing to let me try out as a "walk-on"—in other words, without a scholarship.

The only ounce of encouragement that resulted in this interaction was Coach Kline's willingness to look over my resume and a video of my golf swing. She wasn't making any promises, but she seemed to appreciate our tenacity in reaching out to her.

While this might seem promising to some, the reality was that I was just a girl, who was mediocre at best as a college golfer. The most recent golf swing video I had was from high school, my resume had no updates that were worth noting, and despite my current scholarship, I rarely scored well enough to travel with the top five girls on our team. To me, the situation seemed hopeless. It seemed like I would be stuck in Lubbock, continuously fighting the villain in myself for the foreseeable future.

Prayer request number one felt impossible.

Because there was little else to do but wait, I did my best to have faith that whatever was meant to happen would happen, while also trusting that God would help keep me from running back to Spencer in a moment of weakness. And after waiting a few weeks to hear back from Coach Kline, my mom decided that it was time to check in with her.

"Hello Coach, this is Anne Jones. I spoke with you a couple of weeks ago about my daughter?"

"Oh yeah, I remember you. Funny story, actually. I just ran into a guy from Graham out at a golf tournament. I told him I just spoke to a woman from Graham who has a daughter that would like to play for me ..."

The moment she got off the phone with Coach Kline, my mom's fingers flew over the dialpad.

"Leanne, you are not going to believe this! I just called the UNT coach to check in with her. I barely said hello, and she immediately spoke about meeting Mr. Roberson. Do you remember him?"

"No, who's that?" I asked as I picked a piece of fluff off my comforter.

"He's the one that played golf with Dad," she urged.

"Huh," I replied. I faintly remember the man. He was tall, with the low and slow golf swing.

"Anyway," she continued, "she met him and said that he went on and on about our family being so wonderful and that Dad was a good coach, and that you were great, and then—are you listening to this Leanne?" she asked, her voice rising with every sentence.

I indeed was listening as my feet swung off the bed, sitting upright in anticipation of her next words.

"She said, 'You know I normally don't do this, but I would like to offer Leanne a scholarship for next year. A 75 percent scholarship is all I have. Would that work to get Leanne to UNT?'"

My jaw dropped down so low that it felt like it could hit

the floor. "Shut the front door!" I yelled.

"I told her you'd take it."

"Mom, this is insane!" I blurted out. "God must have hit Coach Kline in the head with a crazy stick! There is no reason on earth she would go from an unwavering 'Not going to happen' to a 'Sure, how about the exact dollar amount needed' in two weeks' time!"

I didn't know whether I should have shouted for joy or fallen on my knees. While my need for a transfer of schools and scholarships seemed impossibly unreachable, God simply stuck out his hand, moved the pieces, and began to place me exactly where I belonged. He knew that I needed an act of God to keep me from falling back into the same old patterns, and even as I struggled through loneliness, I clung to this movement of God in my life. I had to cling to His character, trusting that God was who He said He was. I had to believe that if I would simply submit, if I would simply give Him my story, He would weave it into the most beautiful adventure I could ever imagine. I had to trust Him with my future if I wanted to get away from my past.

And in that moment, in this seemingly impossible situation, God opened up the first massive door to a new life in Denton. He was moving, and as the first prayer request was checked off of my list, the wind began to blow. I could feel it. Rain was coming.

• • •

Lord, I need to be released from my golf contract at Texas Tech in order to accept the University of North Texas scholarship.

After God had moved in such a big way financially, I outgrew the boundaries I had placed on my faith these past two years. I began to believe that if God could bless me with a golf scholarship based solely on a chance conversation, then my other prayers could be answered just as miraculously. I knew that my faith was shifting. The dry season of faith that overwhelmed me these past two years was now being saturated with God's love. Now was the time to step out in boldness and trust that He would answer my second prayer: to be released from my current golf scholarship contract at Texas Tech, which meant asking my current coach for a release from the team.

While this wasn't entirely unheard of among college athletes, it also wasn't an easy conversation to have. But shortly after receiving the news from Coach Kline, the courage to ask for a meeting with the head coach grew alongside my faith.

I had known Coach Mitchell, the head Texas Tech coach, for over two years. And, while he and I had a pretty good relationship, sitting in front of him, knowing I was about to ask to be released from a contract that gave me thousands of dollars, still made my stomach upset.

"So what did you want to talk to me about, Leanne?" he asked, glancing out the window that overlooked the stadium.

"Um, while I am not disappointed here at Texas Tech, I don't feel like this is the right place for me at this time, and I was hoping to be released from my contract," I said calmly. At that moment, I should have been worried, but a feeling of peace washed over me as the words flowed from my mouth.

He sighed. "Leanne, I understand. I want you to thrive both athletically and personally. You go where you need to."

I stood up from my chair, not in disbelief this time but in excitement and wonder at God's love for me. Unable to hide a smile from my face, I hugged him. "Thanks, Coach."

"And you better keep that golf swing straight!" he called as I practically ran out of his office.

Scholarship. Check.

Release. Check.

I could see the door to Denton opening wider than the drive-in movie screen back in Graham. Even as my faith in God grew, I remained in awe at His hand orchestrating every move as if He was playing chess and we were merely the pieces. He knew the full story, but I had realized that my part to play, my role, was to simply let go of the past and trust Him with my future, a future that held another more beautiful opportunity on the other side. Hope continued to build, like rain clouds rolling in, and while I was still in Lubbock, it began to feel less likely that I would stay here.

• • •

Lord, help me find someone to take over the lease at this apartment in Lubbock.

It's interesting how much of our lives can feel bound by contracts. My entire list of prayers was about being released from or entering into some form of written agreement. And the lease on my apartment in Lubbock was no exception.

April, my roommate, ran on the track team for Tech. She was friendly and easy going, so we didn't have a hard time getting to know each other the year prior. When it was time to plan for next year's lodging, I learned she had a boyfriend, with whom she spent all her free time, and that she was looking to get out of the dorms and into an apartment. She wanted more freedom, and to be honest, I couldn't blame her: so did I. At the time, we were a perfect match for roommates, and after basically begging her, we'd signed a two-year lease.

Our lease was on a simple apartment just south of campus. The arrangement seemed ideal, and April was a great roommate because she was kind-hearted and tidy. However, when she said she spent most of her time with her boyfriend, she was not kidding, and this would explain another part of my loneliness my second year at Tech. No roommate chats, and many, many more walks around Walmart by myself.

Fast-forward one year, and here I was trying to get out of the roommate agreement that I had wanted so badly in the first place. Inside, I felt like a jerk. I could anticipate April questioning me while guilt swallowed me whole: "How am I going to make rent without you here?" she would ask. I cared about her and didn't want her to struggle, but I also knew that if I was going to follow God's lead, I needed to confront the next obstacle in my path to Denton. It was just a matter of working up the courage to do so.

For weeks, I anxiously waited for the right moment to share my upcoming plans with April, and on an ordinary Thursday night, the opportunity presented itself. While hanging out on the well-worn beige couch we had found at a garage sale, I explained to April how the Lord had opened the doors for me to transfer. But I also opened my heart with the worry I had in breaking our contract.

"Seriously, April, I was stressing over how to tell you this whole time. I don't want to leave you without a roommate for the next year. I am so sorry!"

Laughing, April looked over at me and said, "You're not going to believe this, but one of the girls on my track team was *just* asking me if I knew of anyone looking for a roommate because she needed a new place to live."

"Get out!" I laughed.

Three prayers down, three to go, and I could feel the slow intermittent raindrops splash on and around my umbrella of faith.

• • •

Lord, if I am going to move to Denton, I need a roommate to share an apartment with. I can't afford a space of my own.

I only knew one person who lived in Denton, and that was a guy named Shane, someone whom my brother Marcus played junior golf tournaments with in his younger days. However, I did not have his phone number and was way too shy to embark on the necessary reconnaissance mission required to get his number. Remember, this was 1996; I couldn't just look him up on Facebook or google his name on the internet! But my mom, who never seemed embarrassed about anything, decided to tackle this obstacle. And after systematically going through a list of twelve different names in the phone book, my mom made contact with Shane's father.

Shane's dad kindly pointed us in the right direction and provided us with the number we needed to reach him in Denton. Feeling awkward and a little excited, I called Shane, a University of North Texas golfer. After a few uncomfortable moments of explaining how I had tracked him down, I shared with him my story of wanting to transfer to UNT and how God had answered my prayers so far. I told him that I needed a roommate for next school year and asked if he knew anyone.

Shane replied, "Well, actually, I don't talk to many girls about their living situation and if they need a roommate. It tends to come across as a bit creepy."

I laughed. "Well, if you happen to hear of a girl at your church that mentions needing a roommate, will you give her my phone number?" I understood he couldn't go around stalking girls for me, but a girl could hope for a chance conversation!

While he was doubtful he would just overhear a conversation about that specific topic, he agreed to let me know if he heard anything. And thanking him, I knew I had to simply leave it in God's hands.

Two weeks later, Shane called me and said, "You're not going to believe this, but I just gave a girl a ride to church, and she said she had to move because of bad roommates. She was pretty distressed about it, so maybe that's your in."

And there was God moving the pieces into place once again.

A few weeks later, the girl, Lindsay, and I met face-to-face on my second trip up to Denton. She was a thin girl with long brunette hair and green eyes. Lindsay grew up in Austin, which is home to the University of Texas, or UT for short. During our time together, we talked about what we wanted in a roommate and where we might possibly want to live, as well as our money restrictions and our personalities. After this conversation, Lindsay told me she would pray about whether or not this was the right fit for her because she did not want to make the same mistake she did with her last roommates.

"There are too many bitches in my apartment right now," she told me.

"Um, what?" I asked, feeling caught off guard.

"Sorry, it's just that my current roommates have two female dogs, which destroy everything. They chew, pee, poop, you name it. Nothing is sacred there. Sometimes my word choice reflects my frustration."

I had to laugh, and immediately I knew that Lindsay was going to be my roommate because of her gusty, matter-of-fact personality.

For Lindsay, however, our weekend in Denton wasn't quite enough time for her to be sure about me as a future roommate. While she and I got along well, after her previous experience, she felt like she needed to know me a bit more before making that commitment. She wanted to make sure it was a God thing first. After our time together, Lindsay drove to Austin to spend some time with her family. That Sunday, as she attended church, she caught up with some old friends, sharing with them that she met a girl named Leanne Jones who plays golf and was interested in being roommates.

Mrs. Harper, Lindsay's long-time family friend, stopped her mid-conversation and said, "You won't believe this, but her brother, Marcus, lives in the house across the street with Cory. Her brother is one of the top golfers at UT!"

In that moment, the realization of what God was doing hit her like a ton of bricks. Lindsay had been friends with Cory for years and had even been over to his house multiple times but never when Marcus was home. Excited, she ran down through the church aisles looking for Cory, and as soon as she found him, she blurted out, "Where's your roommate, Marcus?"

Bewildered, Cory introduced them, and Lindsay's first words were "Hello Marcus, I'm going to live with your sister next year!"

And the raindrops from God picked up their rhythm, growing louder, bigger, and more powerful.

. . .

Lord, I need to get an apartment for the fall in order to make moving to Denton work.

While I went to great lengths to find a roommate, we didn't have a place yet, and we needed one we could afford. Lindsay already had an apartment in Denton with two other girls and a few too many dogs and needed to find something cheap, so we set out to find our new home with the understanding that our pickings might be slim.

The apartment building we found was subpar compared to some of the more sophisticated places in the area, which had pools and recreational activities just steps from your front door. In fact, most people passed this option by because of the lack of activities and location. But I knew many things worth being part of come in odd packages.

The apartment available had neighbors that had a sign on their door with the saying "Have Gun, Will Shoot." And while some might have felt uncomfortable or fearful moving into a place like this, I felt at ease.

More than the place being completely affordable, it had a Denton address. Which meant when I signed the papers ...

I would have a Denton address too.

And as surely as God made it rain to water the seeds on the earth, he was making it rain to water the mustard-sized seed of faith I held in my heart.

• • •

Lord, please help me to find a summer job so I can swing the down payment on our apartment.

I'll admit that I love to see God move in huge and insurmountable ways. Getting my scholarship at UNT was huge. Being released from my Texas Tech scholarship was huge. Finding a roommate in a city I had never lived in was huge. The rainstorm had been prayed for, and my faith continued to grow with every drop.

But then there was this need for a summer job. This prayer seemed smaller than the others, because nearly every student needs a job. But this was slightly different. I needed money for the down payment on the apartment Lindsay and I were supposed to get. But I didn't have it. No down payment, no apartment.

The trouble was that finding a good paying job in Graham for the summer seemed impossible. Since it was a small town, there were very limited options. So I either needed to sign up to work in a fast food restaurant or work at Walmart for minimum wage. It would take a while to make what I needed for the apartment, but, hey, it was at least something.

As I was returning home for the weekend to begin applying, I saw a "Help Wanted" sign in a new store—a local children's boutique. Something moved me to turn my car around and walk in to inquire about the job.

"How may I help you?" asked a woman in her early forties with curly blonde hair and a scarf wrapped around her neck.

"Hi, I'm here for the summer and looking for a job," I answered. "I have my resume here."

"You are prepared!" she smiled, looking over my resume. "I'm Mrs. Grant." She held out her hand and shook mine. "Do you have time for an interview now?"

I was a bit shocked but covered it quickly. "Um, yes, ma'am! I'd love to!"

Come to find out she was the owner and a Christian, and the more we talked, the more she was interested in learning about my future move from Texas Tech to the University of North Texas. She saw my heart and willingness to follow the Lord and encouraged me to do so. After our interview was over, without hesitation, she gave me the job on the spot.

This season in Graham for the summer brought with it some incredibly exciting times for moving forward, but it also brought with it a season that I don't want to admit. After a couple of weeks of being back in Graham, I received a phone call from Spencer. I explained to him that I was on a new path and that I did not want to talk to him again. But he was persistent, and after two more weeks of calling and stopping by my work, I fell again.

Hate might be the best word to describe how I felt about myself during the next six weeks that was left of summer.

Many times I would confide in my boss about Spencer

and my move to Denton, sharing that I knew it was going to be my breaking-free moment, my new start. During my lunchtime at this children's boutique, I picked up a book called *Your Knight in Shining Armor*, by P. B. Wilson. This book changed my entire relationship with God. Reading this book, I felt like I had missed out on so much time with God as I struggled to sort through the mess I created with Spencer again. This book was leading God and me back together. One of the main encouragements was for women to commit to God, to put Him first, and to see what happens next, specifically by committing six months to God without dating anyone else.

Creating this space was intended to help women truly realize that they needed God to save them more than a fairytale prince.

My work was a safe place for me to express my feelings, and even though I did not tell Mrs. Grant the extent of my physical relationship with Spencer, I still shared with her how I felt this relationship with Spencer was toxic for me. It was a bad habit that seemingly I couldn't let go of! She was direct and told me I needed to take that six-month commitment seriously. As I heard her words, I had faith that, as all of my other prayers were answered, God would give me the strength to keep the six-month commitment. He was strong enough to fight this battle for me. And so, with a black permanent sharpie, I signed the six-month agreement in the back of the book, trusting that the villainess I used to see was vanquished by my Savior.

My summer job was over on August 1. I had enough money in my checking account to use for the down payment on my apartment in Denton. I had money to pay for things like gas, door mats, a shower curtain, and an organizer rack with the word "HOME" that hung on the wall. Most people wouldn't think that an organizer rack would have been a big deal, but it was to me. There was something about it that symbolized not just a change in location. It was a change in my life. This last answered prayer was multifaceted. It was not just a summer job. It was a new book. A new mentor. And a new six-month commitment.

And this prayer was the one that brought the deluge of raindrops so overwhelming that I was soaked in His everlasting love and help in my time of need.

• • •

The warmth of the Texas breeze swirled around me like a breath of fresh air as I packed everything I owned into my car. I had spent the last weekend I ever would with Spencer, tying up the final loose end that clung to my old life, our relationship. As I broke things off with him and I closed the trunk of my car, I remember the peace and excitement that surged through my being. It was the first time in a long time that a weight wasn't heavy on my back, dragging and ultimately pulling me back into the depths of my sin. And as I climbed into my car, as I made this new drive, for the first time in a long time, the peace I felt didn't come from the stillness, from the space in between; it came from the anticipation of what lay ahead. A new landscape was on the horizon, a new journey was beginning, and I couldn't wait to get there.

There was something about this shift in my life, this blessing that God had just granted, this second chance that I had just been given that cracked me open in the most beautiful way. I began to understand how God doesn't just work in our lives, but He works in His time. And I also needed my own time. I needed time to make my mistakes. I needed time to drift in the discomfort of "in-between." I needed time to find my way back. And now it was time to let go of my past so I could walk into my future. And as I saw the skyline of Denton emerge into view and all of my past fall into the rearview mirror, I felt the chapter end on that part of my life and a blank page emerge for the story that lay ahead. A story of love. A story of hope. A story of redemption.

A story not shaped by fairy tales but something so much better: a story entirely written by God's great hand.

Nine
Dating God

> By the grace God has given me,
> I laid a foundation.
>
> —*1 Cor. 3:10 (New International Version)*

THE THING ABOUT RAIN IS THAT IT TOUCHES EVERYTHING ALL AT ONCE, and my move to Denton felt like the most beautiful of downpours. Everything in my life was being refreshed and renewed, and I could tangibly feel it changing. I believed I had finally been planted and all of this rain was starting to make things grow. However, even in the midst of my joy, I still could feel overwhelmed at times. And as my faith continued to expand, as I saw His hand in my life answering prayers, giving me grace, and planting me in good soil, one day out of desperation, I decided to ask for something new.

I prayed for rain. Actual rain.

I prayed for it knowing that someone else out there might be praying for sun, and I prayed for it knowing that it would not just rain for me but for everyone standing beneath the clouds.

But I prayed anyway.

Life in Denton was a gift, but between classes and golf and the day-to-day tasks of life, I was beginning to feel weighed down.

On this specific Monday night, I got home at eight p.m. I still had three to four hours of homework, which was due for my two morning classes the next day. I knew this was going to be a late night and the next day would keep up the same pace. By eleven a.m. the following morning, I would be done with class, and a mere two hours later, I would need to be at the golf course, ready to play an eighteen-hole qualifier in hope of making the traveling team for our next tournament.

None of this included the fact that I still needed to pay bills,

and do my laundry,

and answer emails,

and clean the apartment,

and find time to shower.

To be honest, I felt like I was drowning. Sinking, as my growing list of things to do held me beneath the surface. So that night, after finishing all of my schoolwork, I caved under the unbearable pressure I felt and cried. And then I did the only other thing I knew how to do: I got out my prayer journal and prayed.

Dear Lord,

I know You see me. And I want to ask You for something, but I feel pompous even bringing it up. But You, God, already know what's inside my head, so here goes ...

Will you make it rain tomorrow so I don't have to play golf? And since I'm really asking for something big here, can you actually make it rain after my morning classes? The weather channel said there was a 20 percent chance of rain tomorrow. That does not make me very hopeful, but You Lord, You can turn that 20 percent into a 100 percent ... I know You can. Only You control the winds and the waves, so you are the only one I can ask to grant me my request. Oh my God, please! Just please, so I can get a few things knocked off my to-do list. But if not, if your answer is no, I get

*that too. What if someone else is praying that it will
not rain tomorrow? What do You do then? So, Lord, if
it doesn't rain, will You please give me a good attitude
tomorrow, will you give me endurance to get through
the day because I know the day is going to be hard.*

Thank You, Jesus ... I give tomorrow to YOU! Amen.

The next day, I went to my morning classes. No rain. Not even a cloud in the sky.

Later that morning, I went home to eat lunch. No rain.

Around noon, however, as I looked up, storm clouds began to roll in from the North, darkening the skies.

The phone rang and it was my coach. "Big storm is coming in, golf is cancelled today. Take this time to catch up on your schoolwork. We'll be back at it Wednesday."

Just as I hung up the phone, I could hear the soft patter of the rain hit the outside of my window.

I immediately grabbed my rain boots and bolted outside. I ran down the street and around the block to the park that was not too far from our apartment. The temperature had cooled down, lighting flashed in the distance, and the rain turned from a light sprinkle to hefty drops splattering on the earth. It was *raining.*

As I danced with every raindrop that hit my face, I praised the God of heaven! "Thank you!" I yelled with my face turned upward, as the rain kissed my cheeks. I laughed as my tears of joy intermixed with those drops of rain. Because I was in awe of what God had done for me.

Even if two hundred thousand other people had prayed for rain that day, I felt as though this rain was just for me. It was personal. God was personal. And God made me feel as though I was His favorite.

This is who I had become.

I had become a girl of great faith who believed that God would hear and God would listen and God would answer.

I had become a girl who believed that God would make it rain.

While I had reconnected with God, I knew that building a community of friends to support me and help encourage this life choice would be an essential component. Lubbock had been one of the loneliest times in my life, and I recognized that in many ways I contributed to that feeling. Which meant that I also had to acknowledge the ways I would contribute to changing it this time around.

It was during those early weeks in Denton that I created my first real circle of friends, and to this day, they are the friendships that remained. Lindsay was my closest friend in proximity and in my heart. Kee was an over-the-top extrovert who was tall, feisty, and loved playing basketball with the boys. She lived life to the fullest, and her ability to get groups together to play ball or go dancing drew me in right away. But my third closest friend was Whitney, a small girl with dark hair and a bigger-than-life laugh. It was with her that I deepened my commitment to God over reading a book together.

"I really don't want to be boy crazy right now in my life. I want to focus on the Lord," Whitney said as she played with a piece of her curly hair.

"Oh gosh, I have the book for you! It's called *Your Knight in Shining Armor*! I read it this summer, and it was so great. If you want to go through it, I will read it with you."

Whitney agreed with a smile, and we planned to read a chapter and then meet every Tuesday at my apartment to discuss what we had read that week. It was during one of these discussions that I realized that for me, a six-month sabbatical from dating didn't feel like enough time. And as I contemplated this commitment, a number, a specific amount of time kept rushing to the forefront of my mind.

Three years spent tangled in my mess with Spencer.

Three years being torn between the dueling forces of the world.

Three years deeply struggling to connect with God.

I knew I wanted three years to fall in love with my God, my Creator, my Savior once again. As that strong desire filled me, I turned my six-month commitment into a three-year devotion for the purpose of deepening my relationship with God and finding out what He wanted for my future. I trusted that at the end of this time God would bring me "That Guy," the one I had written about in my journal so long ago. The one I had prayed for. Making that choice resurfaced an excitement about God within me the way it did back when I was a child admiring the youth pastor's wife with the Jesus glow for the first time. I wanted that connection again. I wanted that relationship again. I wanted that glow.

And so I pledged my heart into His hands for three years instead of six months.

By mid-autumn of that year, I had thrown myself into my new life with both feet. My heart was filled with exhilaration, gratefulness, and possibility. Everything about this season in my life felt like a revival to me: I had begun to enjoy going to classes again, I had a full blossoming social life with my three close friends, I had a church home that I loved, and for the first time in a long time, the picture I had of myself in my mind was finally beginning to change.

While I absolutely adored all of the friends I had made, my roommate Lindsay and I had a special friendship. We simply began to treat each other as though we had been friends our entire lives. We both loved the Lord, and her humor was right up my alley, making the saying "laughter is the best medicine" so true as it worked to heal the loneliness I had caught in Lubbock.

She was an art major and one semester had a class on anatomy for figure drawing, where she had assignments to draw models wearing only a smile. During this semester she would practice drawing Greek sculptures, like *Discobolus*, also known as "discus thrower," a nude male Greek athlete throwing a discus. One night Lindsay came home from an art convention with a mini picture of *Discobolus*, and this little "naked man" gave us some full belly laughs. When Lindsay showed me that two-inch-sized buck-naked Greek male, I sarcastically told her that I wasn't really comfortable with her bringing a naked man home unannounced.

The next day I grabbed my jacket and took off to my first class. I had gotten all the way there before I noticed Lindsay had pinned the "naked man" to my jacket. I couldn't help but giggle as I unpinned him and put him safely in my pocket.

After that day, the "naked man" was hidden and passed back and forth between Lindsay and I for years. Finding the "naked man" was like finding a treasure chest full of amusement, which was shared with another human.

In a lot of ways, my friendships and experiences in Denton were bringing a new awareness to how I saw myself and how God sees me. It was clear to me, though, that even in this new place, even with a renewed heart for God, there were still things about myself that I needed to work through, things I was ashamed to share, walls that I had built over the years and that still needed to crumble. However, as God likes to do, he began to break down those walls.

I had moved here to escape my past, but because I still had so much shame over my former life, I continued to hide my relationship with Spencer if anyone asked me about my dating history. I wanted to be perfect. I wanted to forget. I wanted to be free from that past life. Nobody knew my real story, and in some ways that made me feel safe. Knowing that this life was completely separate from my past gave me some type of comfort, but I also felt inauthentic in the relationships I was building in Denton. They didn't know all God had done in my life. They didn't know all that he had brought me through and all that he saved me from. They didn't know all of me because I was hiding behind lies regarding my past, and the more I lied, the heavier the weight felt.

Until one night, while Lindsay and I sat on the floor of our apartment surrounded by books and papers for school, I decided to stop pretending.

I told Lindsay the secret I had kept locked deep inside my heart.

I told her about Spencer.

I told her about our toxic relationship.

I told her about my failures and my poor decisions.

I told her I had lied to her. A lot.

I told her I had never confessed these things to anyone besides God before.

I told her I was sorry.

Confessing out loud to another person, putting your sins, your mistakes out there can be really hard. While it is true that my confession to God forgave me of my past sin, by lying to others to hide my past, I just heaped up more sin, ultimately taking away from the beauty of God's saving grace, the glory of his healing, and the weightlessness of a new life in Him. I was missing out on the true gift of these friendships because I was still choosing to hold onto a part of my past. And the weight of these lies grew into a burden that grounded me and strapped me down, keeping all that God had for me.

And as my tears poured throughout this confession to Lindsay, a floodgate also opened in my soul. Soon the pain that was stored up came rushing forth, as though I had burst at the seams and my insides were spilling out. Lindsay heard me, saw me, and forgave me. She hugged me, cried with me, and she loved me despite my shortcomings.

His gifts of grace and mercy were there for me, but to truly receive them, I had to do something that made me uncomfortable, that shook me up a little bit, that required me to shed some of that dead weight I had been carrying so that I could truly be made new.

After my confession to Lindsay about my past with Spencer and the continued failure to tell the truth, my mind had refocused on my new goal in life, which was to fall in love with Jesus. I wanted to give the Lord my whole body, mind and soul. My three-year commitment was a massive part of who I was now and where I had come from. And as Lindsay and I sat drawing on the floor, I used this time as an opportunity to commemorate this renewed relationship with Jesus. I took my pencil and started to outline the silhouette of my naked body down the side of a white sheet, filling it with curves and dark shadows. This piece of art bared not only my body but all of the things that shaped the journey of who I was and the scripture that covered me in grace.

My journey from where I was to where I sat that day.

My journey to find Jesus.

And my journey to find myself.

At first it was simply to pass the time, but as each stroke

of my pencil hit the paper, I began to immerse myself into this work, pouring everything out that I didn't know how to say but all that I *felt* I had become and all that I wanted to be. Those etched lines began to create the visual of all God had done in my life and all that I believed He would continue to do.

A heavy black chain around my silhouette to illustrate breaking from my cycle with Spencer and running to Jesus to be my love, my Savior, my everything. "For your Maker is your husband—the Lord Almighty is his name" (Isa. 54:5, NIV).

An anatomical heart with electrocardiogram lines beating out to represent my new heart, my new life, my new plan, and my desire to guard my heart until the Lord gave the key to my future husband. "Guard your heart ... for ... it is the wellspring of life" (Prov. 4:23, New Heart English Bible).

A beautiful butterfly to express that, with Christ, I felt like I could fly. "If the Son sets you free, you will be free indeed" (John 8:36, NIV).

A perfect globe to remind me of who I was in Jesus, to remind me that I was an overcomer and the things in my past such as my struggles with dyslexia, my insecurities, and doubts would never own me. "In this world you will have trouble. But take heart! I have overcome the world" (John 16:33, NIV).

These images—the world, the wings, my body—these were depictions of who I was. This drawing, this paper filled with multiple illustrations, was what I called "My Self-Portrait," and it was something that I cherished so deeply. Seeing it brought even more healing to my soul. First the confession, now this. It was a reflection of who I saw my new self to be, and I desired to live by its overarching theme. "But by the grace of God I am what I am, and his grace to me was not without effect" (1 Cor. 15:10, NIV).

No one ever really noticed this self-portrait, which I

had framed and hung on the wall, because to most it was just a drawing. But to me it was so much more. It brought about a realization in my heart that I was not expecting. This self-portrait was how I truly saw myself, filled with all of the things I had once wanted to erase about my past and all of the things that I was now. But I didn't erase them. Rather, I drew them in alongside God's forgiveness as they became a piece of His redemption story.

What I also came to see was that the portrait of my life, the portrait that God was creating and molding of me, was ongoing. It was one whose lines and shapes, curves and shadows all made up a bigger picture. And I realized that embracing all of the parts of my story, all of the parts, even the broken parts of who I currently was and who I previously was, allowed God's story of forgiveness and redemption to shine brighter than any perfect picture could.

Ten

That Man

By his grace he gave us eternal
encouragement and good hope.

—*2 Thess. 2:16 (NIV)*

OD HAD USED PEOPLE IN REMARKABLE WAYS TO BRING
ME CLOSER TO THE PERSON HE HAD ALWAYS INTENDED
ME TO BE. While I had been shattered to pieces by my relationship with Spencer, through God's grace and encouragement, I was finding new life in the community I had created
with my church and friends. I was learning about conviction,
confession, and connection in ways that I had always wanted
to experience.

But there was still a part of me that needed to grow, and it
was the part of me that had been shattered the most: my heart.

The reality for me now was that my three-year commitment to God would end and I would find myself back on the
dating scene—a thought that both frightened and excited
me. I trusted that God would place the right guy in my path,
but there was still a part of me that felt resistance to letting
someone back in. Because of that, I used my three-year commitment as an opportunity to pray fervently for "That Guy"
with every passing male that caught my eye. And as I weaved
these prayers throughout my three years of growing up, I began to understand that in this season, my future husband was
also growing up himself. So it seemed only fitting that he
needed a name change too. "That Guy" became "That Man."

I knew that as the prospect of meeting That Man was growing closer, I may have had some uncertainties about giving someone my heart again. This season of dating God felt so safe because I knew that my heart was in the hands of my Savior, but I also believed that God wanted me to experience a relationship with a man on this side of eternity. However, as I observed some seemingly faithful Christian couples, I saw they had broken relationships that would sometimes end with broken hearts. Seeing this created anxiety in my heart, bringing one of my deepest fears to the surface. Despite the fact that so much positive change had happened in my life, there was a nagging whisper telling me that there was no hope for me to experience that fairy-tale ending anymore. I wasn't sure if my past sins had already paved that road for me. I wasn't sure if That Guy would have the chance to become That Man.

But as the three years continued, God's redeeming love showed me time and time again that my story is never over, that new beginnings are what He does best. And, like most classic fairy tales, there are villains to conquer, a princess to rescue, and a happily-ever-after with the prince at the end of it all.

I conquered my villain.

I was rescued by my Savior.

I was ready for my happily-ever-after.

But before my prince would come, God and I still had a mountain to climb. I had to learn to let God heal my heart. I had to give up the fear that engulfed me and trust that the person he picked out for me was better than anything I could craft out on a list.

As I continually went to God in prayer and chose to spend time in the Word and with Him, my faith that He can make all things new would resound in my mind. He is the great architect, the great I Am, and even if I felt like my heart was in a million little pieces, he was able to put me back together again. So as my three years continued, I felt a little stronger each day, and my heart became whole.

In the meantime, while I did successfully commit to three years without dating, I can't say that I never looked at a guy during that time. I didn't live in a convent. I was still around boys, cute boys I might add, and absolutely still had crushes. There was something safe about a crush. No commitment, just finding out more about them without them even knowing I was into them. It was a baby step for my heart. Plus, each time I found myself with a crush, it offered me new vantage points about men, love, and patience, giving me perspective about what would make That Man into the prince I had prayed for.

The first crush rule I set for myself was the determination to pick the right man. And after Spencer, I had set my mind to never date a younger man again. In fact, I wanted someone older, mature, established. I wanted someone who was done with being a little boy and who was done with playing games. And so my first crush before even moving to Denton was a guy that I had never met before. His name was Brent, and he was the son of the pastor in Delton. I had never seen Brent before. I had never met him before. I had never shared words with him. I just knew the pastor had a son, and since his father's words had shaken something inside of me so much so that I moved to Denton, what better assumption to make than to assume like father, like son.

At that time, we didn't have the internet to lead me on a reconnaissance mission and give me all the details ahead of time, so I needed to allow time to play its part. And that's what it did. Once in Denton, I had told Lindsay I thought I would marry Brent one day; I just needed to meet him, and he needed to meet me. This is when she shared with me that Brent was apparently a bit of a party animal—and not really following in the footsteps as his father. She also brought me up to speed on his dating life, which led me straight to the discovery that Brent was planning on getting engaged to his serious girlfriend.

Lesson #1: Picking a husband before ever meeting him is a big mistake.

Now that Brent was no longer the object of fantasy, I found a new focus of attention, Shane, the guy that led me to my roommate Lindsay and the first person that I met from Denton. Shane was super nice, super cute, and played golf, which obviously lined up nicely for a super crush. This crush also started from a distance, and once I had the chance to share more time with him, an obstacle appeared that I just couldn't hurdle: I was taller than him and, for me, this was a deal-breaker. While God healed me from the insecurities of my height, I also knew it would always be awkward for me and him, especially as his line of sight was not exactly where my eyes were.

Lesson #2: Some of the items on my "That Man" list could bend, while some stayed firm.

While the prospect of Shane was gone, he did, in fact, have a roommate. A taller roommate. Which brought hope back into the picture once again.

His roommate's name was James, and on my first visit to Denton, I could tell right away that he liked me. James was a couple of inches taller than me, with auburn hair and dreamy brown eyes. From the conversations we had to the subtle manner in which he gave me attention, I knew that James and I had potential. James was intriguing and endearing and loved to talk about big dreams and big romance. Two of my favorite things! He shared his desire for elaborate dates and passionate love and fantastic futures. Really, he was an ideal candidate, and there was no denying it. But once I moved to Denton and I saw James again, I had just started my three-year commitment and I had no intention of breaking it.

I shared with James about my upcoming season of devotion, alongside my own future hopes and dreams. I even shared with him a little piece of my history with Spencer and how that had impacted what I wanted moving forward. He knew that I was interested in more than just Christian boys who were simply content to stay boys. He knew I wanted a man. So he asked me the "what if" question that was on his mind: "What if you meet your man during your three-year commitment? Would you break the commitment? Would you believe God wanted you to meet him?"

I answered him boldly, "Then if he is really the one, he will be there at the end of the three years!"

Despite the fact that I found him extremely attractive, I knew that for the time being this door was shut. And as time passed and we saw each other less, James started dating someone else and that dream faded from my mind.

Lesson #3: Your soul mate will wait for you.

As the prospect of James waiting for me disappeared, a new man entered at stage left—Mike. Oh Mike! Muscular, handsome, quarterback of the football team, loved Jesus, and was going to seminary to become a pastor. Mike! Does it get any more perfect than that?

I first saw Mike at the North Texas training gym while he was working out. Mike was around six foot two, with dark brown hair, blue eyes, and let's just say that everyone could tell he hit the weights with great results. Someone had shared with me that he had been the all-star quarterback for the football team and had already graduated in May, which meant that he was older. Check! Not only was he perfect on paper, but I also found out that we attended the same church. To put it bluntly, I was crushing hard on Mike, and I had made up my mind that he was the ideal choice for my future husband. He was the crush to end all crushes.

I knew the Lord needed to bring us together, to develop a friendship in this season of waiting, and to help me to control my feelings as I had three years to go before this pursuit could go anywhere. I was playing the long game and needed to hold onto the patience to go with it. What I didn't take into account, however, was how flustered and shy I would get anytime I was near him. My usual outgoing self was reduced to a blushing, embarrassed girl who could hardly form cohesive sentences in his presence! And this is how our story went for quite a while. I would see him at church, and in a moment of panic, hook my arm in Whitney's, quickly turning us around and walking away. And even though I wanted him to know me and fall for the person I was, I couldn't help but turn bright red and trip over my words and flee anytime he came within close proximity.

However, six months later an announcement was made at church that the young adults were going to Russia on a mission trip over the summer for two weeks and anyone interested in participating should sign up. Since my move to Denton, I wanted to break down walls and be bold for the Lord, so for lack of better words, I was determined to jump

all over that opportunity. Full of confidence about my partic-
ipation, I walked over to the sign-up table only to be taken
aback when I saw Mike standing there holding the sign-up
sheet. My skin flushed, and my heart felt like it was beating
out of my chest. I immediately contemplated turning around,
but Mike caught my eye and said hello, informing me that
there would be an informational meeting next week. And so,
with sweat-filled palms, I grabbed the pen from his hand to
write my name and email down, smiling awkwardly, thanking him and quickly scurrying away.

While I knew I wanted to serve the Lord and believed
that going on this mission trip was in His will, I did begin to
struggle with my motives. I wanted to serve the Lord, but if I
was being honest, I felt like a part of me wanted to go just to
get connected to this guy and have him fall in love with me.

Frustrated and a bit confused, I brought this concern to
God. I wanted to have a pure heart about this trip, so I prayed.
I asked for guidance. And, like always, He delivered, answering me in the form of an older woman at church who had
become my mentor over the past year. During one of our
Saturday morning breakfast dates, she reminded me of the
story of Ruth working in Boaz's field in order to be seen. She
shared that women should certainly not be throwing themselves at men, but there is absolutely nothing wrong with
placing themselves in their line of vision. She also reminded
me that when I went to sign up for the mission trip, I had
no idea that Mike would also be going on the trip. And so I
went to Russia. I followed God's lead while simultaneously
making myself a part of Mike's landscape.

Lesson #4: Seek council from those that have walked
the path before you. They already know how to avoid the
uneven ground.

Once in Russia, I found a way to overcome my awkwardness around Mike, and he and I became good friends. We spent time together sharing the gospel with the Russian people. We spent time together laughing and telling stories late into the night. We spent time getting to know each other on a deeper level. And the more I found out about him, the harder I began to fall for this man I thought was already suited just for me. But at the end of the mission trip, as Mike and I sat beside each other on the bus, he said to me, "My friend Adam said that guys and girls can't be friends because one of them is always interested in the relationship being more romantically involved, but I told him that's not true. Leanne and I are just friends, and there is nothing more than friendship there." My heart sank, and while I tried not to let my eyes expose my true feelings, I just nodded and said, "Yeah, just good friends ... that's all."

Lesson #5: No matter how much you are in "like" with a man, if he's not into you, there's nothing you can do about it.

One of the best benefits of a crush is that even when you let yourself daydream about a relationship that doesn't exist, for the most part you are not torn apart by the breakup of that crush. Instead, you move on to the next person who catches your eye. And after Mike, that is exactly what happened to me.

Next, my heart gravitated toward an older gentleman I had met at church. I was twenty-two at the time, and I believed that I was really mature for my age. Without knowing how old Richard actually was, I made a safe bet by guessing he was thirty. Although as Kee and I hung out with each other in the same group as Richard, we would always joke about hiding our love for NSYNC. If we were going to act like mature twenty-two-year-olds, then boy bands were off the table.

To be honest, eight years difference was totally fine with me. He had a job. He was a businessman. He was not a boy. He loved Jesus. He wore a suit and tie and looked good in it. And I was dead set on dating an older man. After all, it made sense that That Guy had grown up. That Man could easily be thirty now.

Richard and I saw each other on Sundays and at church functions, and, unlike Mike, I tried to place myself in his path as much as possible. Until one day, he asked me how old I was and I boldly said, "Twenty-two."

He laughed and said, "Oh, you're just a child!"

Fire shot through my blood as I declared, "I am not! How old are you?"

He answered, "I'm thirty-nine."

Lesson #6: At some point, age does matter.

These crushes were just that—crushes. And what I really came to learn from these experiences in general was that sometimes infatuations help you to discover what it is that you don't want. And that's vital. But we can't know these things if we don't give ourselves the opportunity to know other people, to open up to other people, to risk getting hurt by other people.

While I hadn't been dating during my three-year commitment, the Lord used these crushes to show me: "By His grace, He gave us eternal encouragement and good hope" (2 Thess. 2:16, NIV).

I had good hope in the fact that all these crushes were good and godly men. Maybe these men were not candidates for That Man, but there was hope because godly men were out there; they may be few and far between, but they are not extinct. Plus, I was still working on refining my list to reflect not just the person that I wanted to share my life with but also the person that I had become during this time. I was different now. I had grown, was healed, and forgiven. This list was no longer about the person that I wanted to find but also about the person that I wanted to be. Because I learned that marriage would never be just about finding the right husband; it was also about being the right wife. And after three years of lessons learned, I now believed I was ready for that.

Life in Denton for those three years was filled with so many moments of beautiful hope and grace. So many reminders of the love that God had for me, so many revelations about who I really was in Him, and so many preparations for the seasons in my life that were yet to come. I knew that God had something bigger for me after my time at North Texas, and so the summer after I graduated I began praying, believing that the Lord would open up a teaching opportunity for me. I had faith that God wanted me to work with students, I had faith that He would find a place for me, and I had faith that it would be at the school where I had done my student teaching—in the Denton public school district.

And just like I trusted, He answered. And I got a job!

Before the school year began in the fall, I sat in our small apartment with Lindsay and Whitney, and I reflected back on the three-year commitment I had just lived, and I knew that God had a purpose and use for the time that I had dedicated to Him and our relationship.

I had three years of learning the Bible under my belt.

I had three years of correction and rebuke, teaching me how to listen to others and apologize quickly.

I had three years of journals filled with prayers that the Lord had been faithful to answer.

I had three years of making deep, binding, spiritual friendships.

I had three years of truly getting to know and falling in love with my Savior Jesus Christ.

And after talking with my girlfriends, I realized that I wanted nothing more than to share all of this with young girls as they entered into their own college years. I desired to walk alongside them, to help them navigate through their own journey, to pour into their lives and help them see the God that I knew, loved, and trusted with all of my heart—knowing with full confidence that He was there with them now, and he would be walking alongside them every step of the way.

I wanted to be God's hands and feet wherever it was that He placed me, and so I began to do two things: I began preparing for my first year of teaching, and I began seeking out the college leaders at my church to see if they needed a Bible study leader for a freshman girls group.

The group's coordinator at my church spoke with me on the phone, telling me that this year they were only doing coed Bible studies but that they had a spot for me if I wanted to take it. My initial response was disappointment because I felt strongly that being in a girls-only study was where I was supposed to be. However, after some time, I felt that the calling to serve was bigger than my determination to lead a girls-only group, and so I told the coordinator I would gladly fill the spot. He encouraged me, saying that I would still have girls that needed spiritual leadership and guidance and that there would be plenty of time for girls-only conversation, prayer, and accountability. And he added that my job would be to assist in the direction of the entire group and then provide spiritual leadership specifically for the girls.

Exactly three years and one week from the day that I signed my commitment to the Lord, in the back of *Your Knight in Shining Armor*, I walked into church to begin my first day with this new study group. And if I was passionate about anything, it was talking to young girls about praying for That Man, waiting for That Man, and growing to be the girl that was ready for That Man.

And just as I walked through to the doors to enter our room, there was my coleader, studiously preparing in the corner ... James, from three years earlier.

Lesson #7: Timing is everything.

Eleven
From Who?

And God's grace was so
powerfully at work ...

—Acts 4:33 (NIV)

I T WAS 11:30 IN THE MORNING ON A FRIDAY.
My classroom was abuzz with students practicing their math problems from the lesson I gave earlier in the period, and I was attempting to help Travis, one of my sweet yet habitually apathetic sixth-graders, count decimal places after multiplying. As we worked together in the room, the intercom popped on and blared, "Ms. Jones, you have a parcel in the office to pick up at your convenience."

I responded with a quick "Thank you" and continued with the day's lesson, attempting to not lose focus on my current work with this group of students. If you've ever had a room full of sixth-graders packed together right before lunch, you know how something as simple as an interruption over the intercom can destroy any forward progress during work time.

As the end of the fourth period came and my little darlings began to get squirrelly, I made one final reminder about studying for their upcoming test and dismissed them for lunch. To be honest, I couldn't wait for the period to end either and for *my* lunch to begin. I wanted to know what it was that had been delivered to me, and so I decided that I would swing by the office, pick up my package, and enjoy opening it while eating my lunch back in my classroom.

As I entered the main office, Mandy, our school secretary, was waiting there with a smile. "I made them call you over the intercom because I'm nosy and I'm dying to find out who sent you these!" she squealed before I had a chance to say hello. She lifted up an enormous vase full of flowers, which were a rainbow of gorgeous colors.

"Oh wow! Are those for me?" I questioned as I took the vase from Mandy, who by now bounced a little with excitement.

"Yes, and here's the card. Please, open it!"

I was just as curious to see what it said, so I took the envelope and opened the small card inside.

"*Praying for you, FROM ME.*"

I repeated the words aloud to myself, trying to make sense of what this meant and who it could be from. Looking at Mandy with wide eyes, I said, "This is so weird, who is 'ME'?"

"You mean, you don't know who this is from?"

"Well, I've got a person in mind that I hope it's from," I added, "but currently I don't have a 'ME' in my life."

"Oh, so you don't have a boyfriend?" Mandy questioned.

"Well, I have someone who I want to be this 'ME'; I just don't know if he's available." I paused. As I looked at the card again, I checked for a name and to make sure these flowers had my name on them, excitedly thinking about who this 'ME' was.

And Mandy, who lived for a good love story, exclaimed, "*Please* tell me when you find out who he is."

• • •

It was September, two months before I received the flowers, when a new season of change began. I had just turned twenty-four years old and had also begun working as the sixth-grade math teacher at Strickland Middle School. I had also been asked to be a coleader for the coed Bible study at church with James, and I had just finished my three-year no-dating commitment with the Lord. I could feel it. I knew God had big plans up His sleeve. I trusted that He would continue to bless me with the desires of my heart, one of which was meeting a God-fearing man to share my life with.

Not only that, but I was sure that I could see how God was weaving my story. It seemed to be too much of a coincidence that exactly three years and one week after my no-dating commitment ended, I began to lead a Bible study with James. It had been over a year since we had last seen each other, but spending time together again made it really easy to fall back in *like* with him. He was handsome, he was older, he was a romantic and a dreamer, and he loved the Lord. All major boxes checked. It just seemed perfect. However, that first night of the Bible study I found out there was one small problem.

James had a girlfriend.

Honestly, there was the initial shock and disappointment when he told me he was dating a girl named Jen. I thought I had God's plan all figured out. However, after I got over my initial surprise, I did what I always do. I prayed.

Sitting down on the floor of my bedroom, I opened my journal and began to write my prayer.

Lord, I love You and I know You are good. You have brought me through the heartache of my past, and I know You can do anything. Look where I am ... right now! My three years have just ended, and then James shows up in this Bible study? I feel like this could be

none other than You who put us together! But James has
a girlfriend. So, I'm gonna do something I've never asked
before with all my crushes. I pray that if it isn't in your
will for James and his girlfriend to be together, please
bring this relationship to an end. I pray in Jesus Name!

After writing this, I sat still in the silence. I knew in my heart that crushing on, and hoping to become romantically involved with, someone who was already taken was incredibly wrong. But in my mind, the timing seemed too perfect. I was so sure. As I wrestled with what I wrote, like a soft whisper, I felt God was telling me to trust Him. So with a heart full of resolve, I did. I trusted Him with the same faith that day when He made it rain for me. I trusted Him with the same faith that rescued me from Graham and brought me to Denton. Like those others, He had this situation in the palm of His hand, and so I decided that I was just going to let Him work it out.

Besides, James and I couldn't date each other right now anyway because the church had enforced a "no dating within the Bible study" rule to ensure that everyone attending was there for the right reasons. So, I had time. We had time. And what better way to get to spend some of that time with James as a friend before we became more than friends. If God wanted us to be together, through that friendship, He would open the doors that he saw fit for us in His timing. I didn't want to concern myself too much with the relationship issue, especially after I had given it to God and I believed He told me to trust Him, so spending time getting to know each other without the complications of a relationship allowed me time to just be me and avoid worrying about whether I was doing the "dating thing" right. I just had to be patient and allow God to work in

His timing and in His way, regardless of the future outcome.

The name of the Bible study James and I were leading was called "Structure," and there were over fifteen of these groups from church. The Structure study was a building block for the Christian faith, and I looked forward to every Tuesday night when we would meet up as a group. Our group's study was held at the church, and there were about twelve of us in all, five girls and seven guys, all of whom came to us from the North Texas campus. Most weeks we would start out as a group, work through scripture or a topical study, and then split up—girls and guys—to go deeper into discussion.

We not only met at the church, but I often hosted Girls' Nights at my apartment to connect and grow together in a less structured way. We would paint our nails, watch *Whose Line Is It Anyway?*, eat takeout, and open up our hearts to each other. Each time we got together, we became closer, eventually opening the floor to share our struggles and setbacks in relationships, with both boys and the Lord. This time together helped me to see these girls in a deeper light, allowing me to find ways to support them through all the highs and lows in this season of their lives. One night, after sharing stories about boys, breakups, and heartache, I talked to them about my love for Jesus and how I decided not to date for three years.

"Oh, I would totally not date anyone, but I keep having guys ask me out, and it would be rude to tell them no," Kelly said as she picked out a bright purple color for her nails.

Holly, her close friend, agreed. They seemed to have had a crush on every one of the guys that James was leading. "Yeah, maybe if Big Boy Bobby wasn't in the other group," she giggled, likely daydreaming about his bulging muscles due to his love for bodybuilding.

"I could do it," Bethany shrugged. "I don't have time to date anyway." I knew she was right because, while attending school, she also worked as a physician's assistant putting in over one hundred hours together.

"I'm already taken," Emma said, shaking her head. She was the oldest out of the group at twenty-two.

I glanced over at Mia, who had already selected her color and opened the top. She was an exchange student from Bolivia. "What about you, Mia?" I smiled warmly.

She shrugged, seeming indifferent about the boys in our group. Getting her to talk was difficult at times since she was shy, but as time wore on, she would open up.

I loved that our group was so dynamic and that one girl was not like the other. Each of them had their own story, passions, and struggles. As the weeks passed, I had the opportunity to support both the girls who were really on fire—so excited about Jesus and what He was doing in their lives, while also being there for the girls who were struggling and scared about being away from home, working through a boy-crazy phase, or dealing with serious struggles. As time passed, it was evident that God's hand had moved me to this group to share my testimony to girls that were the same age as I was when I went through my season of struggle. He used my mess to spread God's message. Of love. Of forgiveness. Of redemption. And it was so beautiful.

James also led the way for the guys to model what it looks like to follow hard after Jesus, work hard in school, and form a brotherly bond that holds firm. However, having a coed group also brought with it an interesting dynamic. While the girls and guys of the group seemed to get along quite well, Emma always complained about a guy a couple of years younger than her, Zach. She would say that everyone in her anatomy class, even the smart kids, would make a thirty or forty on the test but he would make a ninety.

"He's got a photographic memory, and he doesn't even study!" she complained.

"Yeah, but he is super dreamy, being tall, dark, and handsome!" Kelly would say.

I rolled my eyes at Kelly because I had noticed that Zach was well aware of how he looked and the effect it had on girls.

Despite the occasional differences, together, we—the girls and guys—developed a close-knit friendship even in the first few months of our time together, making room for more of Jesus in all of our lives.

Oftentimes churches and Bible study groups would take the opportunity to get away and learn more about the Lord and one another while also enjoying a weekend of fun, games, and team-building. Because my family lived in Graham and had a lake cabin near our house, James and I decided that it would be the perfect place to get away with our students and hold a retreat. So one weekend in November we traveled to Graham, and the girls stayed at my parents' home and the boys took the lake cabin.

I couldn't wait to have a weekend away with my girls to show them my childhood home, to have them meet my parents. And despite the fact that there was a small part of me that felt anxious at the idea of going back to the place that held so much of my history, I was excited about sharing this part of my life with them. The other bonus, of course, was that I would also get the opportunity to spend time with James for the entire weekend, as his time was typically wrapped up with his girlfriend outside of Bible study.

As the weekend commenced, we spent some of our time in small groups working through our study, letting everyone ask the hard questions, and diving deeper into scripture to find answers. But after lunch, we would all meet back up at my parent's house and play. We hit golf balls, played volleyball, asked the "Would you rather—?" questions, and even had a cutthroat round of knockout basketball as a large group.

At one point we had a heated round of Pictionary going, and in true competitive fashion, I rallied my team, which had Zach, Kelly, Bobby, and Holly. It was an ALL-PLAY, which meant one person from each team had to draw, and whichever team guessed the answer the fastest would win! I was up to draw against James. My competitive nature came out, and I could feel the heat in my bones wanting to win.

The card was drawn. James and I both looked at the word and sighed. He turned to me and leaned in close with his lips right by my ear, whispering, "How do you draw that?" Chills ran down my spine, but I eyed my team to be ready. I wasn't going to let a simple crush distract me. No way. This was for the win.

The timer started, and I quickly drew the lines for a top hat. But before I could even get it finished, I heard Zach yell out above the crowd, "Abraham Lincoln!"

"What?" I asked, surprised. "Yes! That's it!"

All the teams stopped screaming at once. James dropped the dry-erase marker and stared at Zach.

And I went bananas!

My team ran around the room giving high fives and shouts for joy! No one really knows how we got so lucky that day, but we won! And it felt good. It felt so good to play, to be in my element, to share more of myself with people that I cared deeply about, to be home in Graham without feeling empty.

Despite the fact that I was still wrestling with my emotions regarding James, I did enjoy the attention that I got from him while there. He often came up to me and gave me great big bear hugs, smiled at me while in conversation with others, or just found a way to give me that extra attention. I didn't want that to be the focus of the weekend, but honestly the more it happened, the more starry-eyed I got. And on the Saturday night of our retreat, during a game of pickup basketball, I found myself daydreaming about him again. I had just gotten benched from the game and replaced by one of the tallest guys in the group, Greg, and so this gave me an opportunity to watch from the outside. And it was fun to watch James—enjoying the company of the group of guys while also playing basketball, a game I loved. He was a sports guy, which made me even more attracted to him because of my own love of sports, and I couldn't help but get all the feels. While I was sitting out, Mia and Bethany walked up to me and, through their giggles, they whispered, "Gee, Leanne, your eyes always seem to follow one person!"

As the realization set in that my crush was not so subtle, my cheeks heated and I quickly became really embarrassed. These feelings had been my little secret (or so I thought), and I knew immediately that I needed to be careful with my words and my actions because James had a girlfriend and everyone knew it.

After this little bout of embarrassment and after everyone else went inside, I decided that I needed to shoot some hoops by myself. I wanted to sit with my feelings again for a minute, to consider James, my heart, and how I was conducting myself. I had prayed, trusted God, and was waiting on Him to move. However, while I wanted to be an example to the girls, in my heart I also wanted James to notice me, to like me, to want to be with me. I wrestled with these feelings as God said to trust Him, and I really didn't want to be the other woman—or to even flirt with that idea. And as I sat with these thoughts, tossing the basketball and hearing the gentle swoosh of the hoop, I heard a voice from behind calling my name.

"Hey, may I join you?"

And, turning with surprise, I bounced the ball in his direction.

"Sure, Zach," I stated, "if you think you can handle losing."

Twelve
From Me

The grace of our Lord was
poured out on me abundantly.

—1 Tim. 1:14 (NIV)

I T WAS ZACH.

Not James, but Zach.

I'll admit, I wanted it to be James standing there in that moment. But it wasn't.

A smirk spread across Zach's face as he accepted my challenge.

"Oh, you like to trash talk?" he replied. "Well, you better have some game to back that up, or you're going to be embarrassed." Zach pulled up for a jumper—the ball clanged off the rim and bounced right back to my hands.

Standing at the three-point line, I let the ball spin out of my hands and swish the net. Leaving my hand in the air with three fingers raised, I said, "Are you sure you want to do this? You know I beat James two games in a row, and it looks like now he doesn't want to play anymore."

"Oh yeah? You may be a better shot than I am, but my strategy is to always outlast my opponent. Let's just say I never give up!"

On the concrete driveway at my parent's house, with chalk lines marking out the boundaries of a basketball court, I relaxed, finding laughter and amusement in this back-and-forth banter.

About thirty minutes later, James walked out and yelled, "Hey, you two, it's time for dessert! Come back inside, we're making ice cream sundaes."

"I guess that makes me the winner!" I boasted to Zach.

With a grin on his face, he replied, "For *now*, but I want a rematch."

That evening, all of us packed up our bags and our fun-filled memories and prepared to head back to our daily lives. It was slow and silent, like friends parting ways after summer camp. As James and I were packing the van, we heard panicked cries coming from one of the other rooms in my parent's house. Bethany was on the ground, shaking and convulsing, having a seizure on the worn hardwood floors.

My parents called 9-1-1, and in a matter of minutes, the ambulance roared down the neighborhood street and took our friend away. We all stood quietly in the driveway as we listened to the sirens fade out in the distance. I felt the cool air blow across my face that comes before a storm, and a rumble of thunder in the distance.

As I looked at the faces of everyone, I could see it. The fear, the uncertainty. And while this weekend was about us pressing into God's presence, we never realized how much we would need it until this moment. Watching Bethany go from a determined girl full of life to a frail body lying on a stretcher had been hard on all of us.

She had been taken to the hospital and remained there until doctors could determine a cause. Meanwhile, the rest of us gathered to continue our weekly study, with a missing piece of our group lying in a hospital bed. During that first meeting after the retreat, James and I announced that we would be heading to the hospital to visit Bethany and invited anyone else who would like to join us. Zach, the only one able to break away from his midterm studies, agreed to meet at my apartment so we could drive over to the hospital.

Bethany looked healthy and had a positive attitude, much to our relief. She was just like the girl we had last seen before she had her seizure. Doctors were beginning to believe stress had been the cause of her seizure, and they were waiting on a couple of more test results before releasing her from the hospital. This made sense as she was the one working over one hundred hours a week in physician's assistant school.

We didn't stay long. Visiting hours were short and after thirty minutes, Bethany, despite her cheerful disposition, now seemed tired and a little withdrawn. We gathered around her, and just like we did on the driveway of my home as she was being carted away in the ambulance, we prayed for her recovery and for God's hand to be over her and her doctors.

For all of the interest I had in James leading up to this time, I was never more grateful for his presence than I was now. I was still shaken by the pain that comes with witnessing human suffering in that way. It felt like a different kind of loss, a different kind of ache, a different kind of gaping hole left in your heart. But right there, standing alongside me in this valley of shadows, was James, a sliver of light. And I might not have been his girlfriend, but I was still his friend. He was here right beside me, and that was a good enough start.

We pulled up to my apartment building and stepped out of Zach's truck. The night air was refreshing after the medicinal staleness that lurked in the hallways of the hospital. I desperately wanted James to stay back with me.

I had no interest in pursuing him, but I just needed space to talk with someone about my feelings. I needed to say them out loud. I needed somewhere for them to land.

But James didn't stay.

He hugged me and slapped Zach on the back as he jumped in his car, waved goodbye, and then drove away. Watching him leave left me with a pit in my stomach. It wasn't until Zach said my name for the second time that I finally snapped out of the moment.

"Leanne?"

"I'm sorry... what?" I replied as my senses were brought back.

"Would it be okay for me to grab a glass of water before I hit the road? Hospitals make me thirsty. I need to drink a lot of water to detox or something."

"Oh yeah ... sure," I said, partially confused and partially trance-like.

Zach followed me through our apartment door. I hung my keys on the "HOME" organizer rack that I bought the summer before my first year at Denton and welcomed him in.

He walked in and looked around as I hung my jacket in the front closet.

"This drawing," he said, staring at my framed self-portrait that I had drawn a few years ago, "it's really interesting! Did you do this?"

Out of the many people who had hung out during our game nights and movie nights, he was the only person that noticed my self-portrait. The otherwise invisible piece of art in our apartment. The visual evolution of all that I was and all I had become.

"Oh, that thang? Yeah, I know that it's not very good, but I really wanted to hang it up because it's important to me," I said.

"Gosh, no. It's beautiful. I mean it," he said. "And say 'that thang' again! I love your accent!"

Immediately my body tensed as flashbacks of middle and high school came back to me. Nobody liked my accent. I felt defensiveness rise within me, and before I could stop myself

I blurted, "You don't love my accent, you're just making fun of me!"

"No, not at all," he responded with a softness in his voice. He turned to me and held my gaze. "I find your accent completely adorable. It sounds like a sweet Southern belle, and I could listen to it all day."

Those words lingered in the air between us, and for a brief moment the conversation made me feel a degree of discomfort; I wondered if he could sense my insecurities and vulnerability.

Is this guy interested in me? No, I'm sure he's not. He's just trying to be nice.

To create distance just in case, I walked around the corner to the kitchen and grabbed a glass out of the cabinet. "Thanks, I guess. I've just never been really fond of my accent."

"Why?" he asked.

I was beginning to be afraid this was about to go beyond a glass of water. "I don't know. I got made fun of quite a bit when I was a kid, and it's always kind of stuck with me, I guess."

"I get that. I have dyslexia, and I couldn't read until I was in the seventh grade, so it was easy for others to make fun of me for that when I was growing up."

"You have dyslexia?" I blurted out, remembering how Emma said he always had the highest grades in class.

"Yeah, funny story. I would tell my grade school teachers that I couldn't see so that I wouldn't have to read off the board in class. Or pretend I had a sore throat and was losing my voice if I was asked to read out loud from a book. Several of my teachers saw right through my deceit, but it was my sixth-grade teacher, Mrs. Brown, who asked to have me tested for a learning disability. It wasn't until I was told I had dyslexia that I really found freedom in my struggle. It gave the struggle a name. And while it did take some time, I've learned that you just gotta own what you've been given, ya know?"

"Sure," I replied.

The truth was, however, that I didn't know. When I was younger, I had never accepted my dyslexia or my strong Texan accent or my many physical curves. I didn't stand tall in my own truths. Instead, I hid them. Yes, I was a fighter. But Zach was bold about his struggles. He was out front, in public. He embraced who God made him to be. And I couldn't quite figure out if that was arrogant or brave. But either way, Zach's confidence at such a young age was thought-provoking. And I was intrigued because he saw it all differently. Where I had seen flaws and challenges, he saw triumph and victory.

I brought him his glass of ice water, condensation forming on the side, and I took a seat on the couch across from him.

"Wow! Your acceptance of having dyslexia is surprisingly mature for your age," I said, trying to fill the awkward silence that had formed between us with a little light-hearted banter.

"My age!" he bounced back, quickly reminding me that he was, in fact, nearly twenty-one.

"Okay, okay, sorry," I said holding my hands up in surrender. "So Mr. 'Nearly Twenty-One,' what are you here for? What's your major?"

"Well," he began, "what I'm here for and what my major is are two different things, but right now I can tell you I'm trying to stay away from my old patterns. You see, I grew up here and I got into all types of trouble before I truly met Jesus."

I let out a deep sigh of familiarity, then opened my mouth to say how I understood all too well, but before I could share in his sentiment, he continued to tell me his whole life's story. I didn't say more than a few words over the next four hours. I just listened.

I listened to him talk about his childhood and how his parents had a pretty unstable relationship, which created tension and made him feel like he was walking on eggshells in his own home.

I listened to him share that in high school he would seek out affirmation from his peers, and because his desire for their acceptance overruled any of the moral standards his parents had put in place, he lived his life for the approval of others.

I listened to him confess that, over time, the feeling of emptiness was filled with substance abuse and sexual relationships.

I listened to him declare that his rock bottom came in the form of a car wreck, after a night of drinking and partying.

I listened to him say that because of that wreck, he had a talk with a gentleman by the name of Brad Bell, who shared with him that God still loved him—right where he was.

And I listened to him tell of how he went to England to study abroad so that he could run away from his old life but that God had brought him back to his hometown. And now he was trying to learn what God had for him next.

Oh, how I understood this cycle of sin, and, right there in my living room, sitting on my well-worn couch, my heart very much felt the place Zach was in. He was me three years ago. He was breaking free. He was starting his pilgrimage, and I felt compelled to encourage him that God would be just as faithful to him as He was to me.

"Zach, you have a great story," I spoke quietly, "and I believe God has so much more ahead for you. You are just starting your journey, so my encouragement would be to hold tight to this group of guys in this Bible study. They will help keep you away from all those old habits."

We let stillness settle in the room for a moment.

"Yeah," he said, "that's my goal. I want to stay as busy as possible. It was hard for me to move back to my parent's house because there are so many triggers in that house, but my plan was a new start in Denton, with the Lord being my main focus."

One glass of water and four hours later, I could see why Zach was still sitting in my living room. He didn't have anywhere else to go. And I felt sorry for him, thinking to myself that he must be terribly lonely.

He's trying to stay away from old habits.

Trying to make new friends.

Trying to be busy with this new way of life.

Trying to grow in his relationship with the Lord.

Trying to be the man God intends for him to be.

Which led him here.

After I had a chance to encourage him, we continued to talk. The more we spoke, the more I realized that this guy, Zach, was a pretty cool kid and that perhaps he and my sweet Mia from our group might enjoy the company of one another. *In fact*, I thought to myself, *they just might be a perfect match.*

As the dust settled on this night, life quickly fell back into its usual rhythm. Except that now I had a new goal in mind: to ensure that Zach and Mia found themselves in the same places at the same times. This meant inviting the two of them whenever Lindsay and I had friends over or whenever we went out in groups. These group outings came with mixed emotions for me, though. On the one hand, I wanted to bring these two people together to see if they would make a good match. But on the other hand, I was still wrestling with my feelings for James, especially because just one week prior I had received flowers at work sent "From Me," really hoping that they were from him. However, despite that hope, he often showed up to these group outings with his girlfriend, leaving me teetering on this spectrum of emotion—somewhere between excitement for my friends and pain over my own aching heart.

During one particular game night, Lindsay and I invited a group of seven friends over to our apartment, including Zach and Mia. We all had pizza and sat around laughing and talking. I had my usual cup of Sonic Ice—my favorite drink—in one hand and a slice of pizza in the other. To get the game night rolling, Kee suggested that we play the fun get-to-know-you game called "Two Truths and a Lie." The object of the game being that, from the three facts presented by any given person, the group had to guess which one was the lie. Of course my competitive spirit wouldn't back down from a game, and I knew I was pretty good at picking out a lie. And as Zach volunteered to go first, I rubbed my hands together knowing I could take the first round.

He stood up at the front of the room with his usual confidence and stature.

"I'm afraid of heights."

"I want gnomes on ponies standing with me on my wedding day."

"I have never been in love."

I knew from our four-hour talk that Zach was afraid of heights, and I knew that he dated a girl name Hailee pretty seriously in high school, but he confessed he didn't love her, so it was pretty easy to see the gnomes and ponies was the lie and just stupid.

"Oh Zach, I've got you pegged!" I declared. "Of course your lie is the gnomes and ponies!"

Zach laughed and said, "Nope, Leanne, you got it wrong. I really want gnomes and ponies beside me on my wedding day. My lie was that I have never been in love."

"What?" I blurted out and stood there, confused and frustrated by his juvenile wedding wishes. I couldn't stop wondering how I missed the part where he had been in love with Hailee.

Lindsay pulled me aside, curled toward the wall, and said, "Zach sure is hanging around a lot. It seems like he is interested in you much more than the games."

"Oh Lindsay," I whispered so no one could hear us, "if you would have heard his story, you would know he just says 'yes' to every invitation so that he can stay busy. And for goodness sakes," I folded my arms, "I'm three years older than him. He's just a child. Did you hear that absurd gnomes and ponies thing? I want an older, mature man."

"Oh, I know you want older," Lindsay reasoned. "What I'm saying is that I think he wants someone older too!"

I wearily let Lindsay talk her way through her stream of thought, all the while knowing that Zach and I would remain simply friends. I had other plans for him on the horizon. Plus, the truth was that I still, in the back of my mind, thought about James more than I would like to admit, and I was waiting for God to move our relationship forward.

Feeling that Lindsay's rant had gone on long enough, I interrupted. "Don't be ridiculous! I'm planning on setting him up with Mia as soon as the Bible study is over and the no-dating rule is dropped. He's twenty-one now, and she's twenty-one; they are in the same season of life. It's perfect!"

As time moved on, my newfound friendship with Zach gave me the comfort to share my raw truths with him and about him. Just in case Zach did like me the way that Lindsay said at the party, I wanted to be honest with him—so honest that he would know I wasn't interested in traveling down any type of romantic road with him. We were just friends. And I tried to make that clear to him from the beginning.

His friendship was good for me, and though I didn't see him as dateable, I enjoyed having someone around who appreciated the person that I was. In fact, it seemed that he welcomed it. He also began to become more of a leader during our Bible studies, and as he shared his heart, time became richer every week that our group got together, generating boldness with other members of the group as well. He was growing, our group was growing, and God was moving. I loved those times together as a group and felt that everything had been put together perfectly. God knew that we all had some growing to do, and he placed the people that we needed in our lives to pull open the shutters on our dark little corners and shed new light.

There was one night at Bible study, however, where God opened my eyes to see the depth of this new friendship, and it caught me off guard. Most of the group had left by this point, but James, Zach, Bethany, and I were cleaning up before we left for the evening. As we all talked about our week's plans, Zach turned to me and casually asked, "Hey, did you get the Sonic Ice I left you before it melted?"

"Oh, that was from you?" I asked, a little surprised. "I thought it was from Lindsay!"

"Nope. That was from me."

I stopped for a moment, questioning if I heard him correctly.

Did he just say "from me"?

Thirteen

The Wall

> My grace is sufficient for you, for My
> strength is made perfect in weakness.
>
> —*2 Cor. 12:9 (NKJV)*

S O, IT WAS ZACH.

He sent me the flowers.

He brought me the Sonic Ice.

He signed the note, "FROM ME."

But what he didn't know was that my heart was hidden deep within the walls I had built around it, and he was not getting in unless the Lord let him.

I have always been so captivated by the phrase "he stole my heart." As a young girl, I often dreamed about that knight in shining armor who would stop at nothing to win me over. To me, this man would be one with unyielding determination, strength, and bravery. He would believe in his heart that even standing against unimaginable evil and danger was worth it to call me his.

Because I didn't want my heart to be taken by just anyone, I entrusted my heart to the Lord, hiding it away until That Man came for it. However, in that declaration, I had begun to build a wall around my heart, and while God was now its keeper, the wall was constructed with the bricks of my past, making it nearly impenetrable to any potential suitors that surrounded me. And even though I may have had crushes, I never really gave my heart away.

Finding a way around those walls of my heart would require patience.

Finding a way around those walls would require prayer.

Finding a way around those walls would require unyielding determination, strength, and bravery.

Finding a way around those walls would require God.

I knew that if someone wanted my heart enough, they would pray for my love. And I also knew that if God was a part of the equation, if He was willing to give my heart away, then my heart would not be a stolen good but a gift that could be fully enjoyed.

And my wall worked well, as long as I could anticipate *who* was coming too close.

But if the last three years of walking with the Lord had taught me anything, it was that healing and change take time. And there were still these giant blocks keeping me from the life I had desired. The hurts and fears of my past, which I thought had been removed, had actually been neatly stacked and aligned in perfect order, creating something solid for me to hide behind. And while God had been so good to me and had brought so many people and situations into my life that spurred me forward, there were still times when circumstances felt like they would never change.

It had been over three months since my commitment to the Lord had ended. The Bible study had started in September, and now it was the start of a new year, January 1, 2000. Our Bible study had rung in the New Year with a party. James kissed his girlfriend as the countdown hit zero, and at this point, I had given up hope that James was the perfect answer to my three-year commitment. However, as my eyes turned away from him, I seemed to have gained the eyes and affections of Zach, someone three years my junior who, though fun and cool to be around, reminded me of who I was three years ago. New in my walk with the Lord, immature in my faith, and in need of serious maturity and development.

I wanted an older man.

I wanted someone spiritually mature.

I wanted someone who had gone through their boy stage and was ready to take on the task of caring for me.

I didn't want to play around in relationships, and I needed That Man to take this seriously.

And while it was obvious that Zach was kind, funny, and continuing to grow, he just wasn't quite mature enough.

However, I also loved having him around. We got along so well together, and so despite the feelings I could see he was developing for me, our friendship continued.

Friendship really is such a funny thing. You are just living life day to day, and then one chance encounter, one meeting, and you decide to let them into your life, to see the bits of you that the rest of the world can't, to invite them into your home and your life like they had always been a part of it.

It was kind of like that with Zach. One day, I wouldn't have even really taken notice of him, and then all of a sudden, most of my days included him in it. And soon, before I even really knew it, he became a part of the fabric of my life. To be fair, Zach did whatever he could to make this happen. It was clear that he wanted to be around, and though at first I thought it was just because he was lonely, I knew now it was because he had a crush on me. Knowing this bothered me a little, but I was still on a mission to bring Mia and Zach together. I thought they would be great as a couple, and because I considered myself somewhat of a matchmaker, we continued to be a part of each other's lives. I knew that I didn't want a relationship with him, and because of this, my attitude toward him created space for me to be completely honest about the things in him that I noticed, both the good and the bad. I knew that if he was just my friend, it wouldn't hurt to speak truth to him, to call him out on his immaturity, and to share the parts of me that a true suitor of my heart wouldn't be privy to until much later on. And so that is exactly what I did.

I remember one day in particular in early February I was walking home from school in the cold, feeling sorry for myself because my car wouldn't start and that, rather than waiting for someone to jump it, I would just walk home.

"I normally don't pick up people from the side of the road, but you look like you might need some help," Zach called out his car window as he slowed down beside me.

With a smirk, I continued walking, sharing with him my decision to walk home because of my car's inability to start. After all, it was only three miles away. In true Zach fashion, he took this as an opportunity to both rescue me and gloat.

"Oh, a damsel in distress. Good thing I have jumper cables. How about we go back to your car, and I'll see if I can get it started?"

I took him up on his offer and was grateful to have help even though I was in a sour mood. We quickly made it back to my eleven-year-old Buick LeSabre, which he so lovingly called the "gray dragon held together with duct tape and super glue," and he started it right up with his jumper cables. Feeling like I should thank him for his help, I suggested we go get hot chocolate as a sign of my appreciation.

After dropping off my car, we drove to Beth Marie's, an old-fashioned soda shop on the Denton Square. As we sat at a table, sipping our steaming mugs of hot chocolate filled to the brim with whipped cream, Zach opened up about his scholarship to study in England at Birmingham. He told me that he had racked up some significant credit card debt while cutting classes to travel all over Europe. So, instead of holding my tongue, I told him how irresponsible it was having credit card debt. I then went on to not-so-gently encourage him to get a job because that's what grown-ups do. He was a student, yes, but again, due to his scholarship, he had never needed to hold a job in order to pay for schooling. And while I shared my honest feelings with him, I could see he was listening.

In one week, he had gotten a job.

In two weeks, he had gotten two.

And before the end of February, he had picked up three jobs, allowing him to pay off his debt quickly and effectively.

He listened. He had true character. He was interesting. His maturity was growing at rates more rapid than I ever imagined. And just like that, my wall had begun to show cracks in it that never existed before.

Many nights during the school year, Lindsay and I continued to have friends over to hang out, play games, or watch movies. I loved that our home became a hub for everyone and that people felt safe and wanted in our space. And so it was no surprise that during spring break on this particular Friday night, all of our friends, including Zach, had come over to watch some March Madness basketball games and eat pizza. Lindsay, who usually was a part of the festivities, had left for the evening to spend time with her boyfriend whom she had been seriously dating for eight months.

After the party ended, and Zach and I were cleaning up, Lindsay burst through the door in tears. Her boyfriend broke up with her, which was a surprise to all of us. She was so sure she would marry this guy, and now she had to tell people he was no longer part of her life. My friend, who was usually so bubbly and full of life, looked completely devastated.

Tears poured down her face, and my heart hurt for her as I handed her a box of tissue. "This breakup has ruined everything," she sobbed. "All the plans we had made together for our future!" And soon the sadness I had felt at seeing her so broken turned to anger and, without thinking, I let my tongue loose.

"Lindsay, I'm so very sad for you—I am. But I told you that I didn't think you should have planned for your future with him when there wasn't even a ring on your finger!"

Lindsay, feeling completely broken, fell to the floor and sobbed desperately. I quietly knelt down beside her and hugged her while poor Zach was stuck listening in the background, not knowing whether to leave or stay.

After a few minutes, when Lindsay got her bearings, I decided to get up from the floor and walk Zach out to his car, doing what I could to rescue him from what I imagined to be an uncomfortable situation.

"Hey, can I say something real quick?" he asked as we walked through the parking lot to throw the trash in the dumpster.

"Sure," I said, glancing up into the night sky.

"Leanne," he said, leaning in gently, "I admire how much you care about Lindsay, and I can see how hurt you feel for her. But in your desire for Lindsay to not get hurt, you come across as arrogant. And I'm sorry to even say that because I think so highly of you."

His words stopped me in my tracks. He was right. I was so afraid for Lindsay to get hurt; I had warned her to build the same walls around her heart as I did mine. And when she didn't listen, when she didn't build them and protect herself, I could feel that old, familiar sting. It was as if I was reliving my experiences all over again, like I hadn't built my own all those years ago and I was lecturing her like I would have myself. Only this time it wasn't me who was hurting. This time she had been the girl fooled, the girl who fell. And in my attempt to remind her not to make that mistake again, I was behaving like I was superior because *I* wouldn't make those mistakes again.

A lump formed in my throat, and as quickly as my pride had swelled up inside me, it fell to the ground like a weight too heavy to carry. Little puddles formed in my eyes, and I spoke with trembling softness. "You are right. You're *so* right, and I was too prideful to see it. I owe Lindsay an apology."

As I headed back inside, I thanked Zach again, and I went to ask Lindsay for forgiveness.

And just like that, Zach's light shone once again. In a moment that could have been very uncomfortable, he chose to help me become a better person. He was willing to open my eyes and bring me face-to-face with my own humanity even if he wasn't sure how I would react. And with his bravery, I felt some of my bricks come tumbling down.

It was only a week after the Lindsay breakup that, as I was getting ready for work, I remember feeling like I was burning up. My throat hurt and my body ached. Quickly I knew I would not make it through a full day of teaching, so I contacted the school to let them know that I wasn't coming in for the day. As I readied my things for a day on the couch, the phone rang and, wouldn't you know it, Zach was on the line. I told him that I wasn't feeling well, that I had a fever, and that because Lindsay was not home, I was going to try and run to the store to pick up a thermometer because, depending on how high my temperature was, I may need to head to the hospital. Zach, however, told me to just stay where I was and said that he would pick up anything I needed.

He made it to the apartment in record time with a bag full of supplies, soup in hand, and came to the couch to help me out. We took my temperature and, seeing that it wasn't dangerously high, I began to nestle in to get some rest. He got me another blanket and some ice water and sat with me for a while before leaving.

He was there for me.

He saw me.

Even in the disheveled, broken-down, rough-looking state of sickness he saw me. And while I was clearly not appealing in either looks or disposition, he looked at me with such gentleness and care that it shook me to my core, taking with it a few more bricks that I thought were so solidly locked in place.

Once I had fully recovered from this bout of sickness, I was ready to get back into the routine of daily life. This school year was really flying by, and spots of green were starting to pop up everywhere—on the ground and in the trees—which indicated that wintertime was over. It was the last weekend in March, and that weekend I really wanted to find something in the area to do that was both fun and entertaining. I had been stuck on the couch for three days, and so when Zach suggested to a group of us that we should go play golf and then go to the Mavericks game in Dallas, I was all in. Not only did I love spending time with my friends, but I also loved basketball and golf, so this was a perfect plan for our Friday.

Zach pulled up in his green Toyota 4Runner with our friend Greg riding shotgun. I hopped in the back seat, and off we went to pick up Kee. While the golf balls were flying all over the course, I got the biggest laugh when Zach shared a story about how his high school golf career had ended. While I had expected a story wild enough to warrant losing his place on the team, what I didn't expect was that it ended with his pants around his ankles while hitting golf balls after losing a bet—on the very same course I was playing on that day for the North Texas team.

Zach, Greg, Kee, and I fell over laughing. Not only was I there at the same course that day, but it came to light that I was the one that outed his indecent exposure. I had been waiting for my other team members to arrive before heading down the driving range when I saw it—a bright white bottom, apparently Zach's bright white bottom. I had told my UNT coach, who immediately alerted the staff.

After that story, there were jokes about Zach being Mr. Confident—the one that can play golf with, or without, clothes on.

After our outing, the car ride home was filled with even more laughter and fun. The friendship between us had blossomed so much over the course of the year. When I began Bible study that school year, I thought I would gain James as a boyfriend and future husband, but instead I got these friendships that were fun and dear to my heart. I almost felt a twinge of sadness about it all ending soon. Would I still hang out with Zach once the Bible study was over? Though I hoped our friendships would remain, I could feel change coming.

As we neared Denton, Zach began to drop each of our friends off one by one. And as each person exited the vehicle, I could feel the air in the car shift a little bit more. Zach had found a way to drop everyone else off before me, and I was sure he was up to something. I just wasn't sure what it was yet.

Before I knew it, it was just me and him in the car. While we had been alone together on a few occasions, for some reason this felt different. Maybe it was because the last interaction we had was at my apartment when I was sick, maybe it was because we were alone in a car together, or maybe it was because of something I hadn't quite admitted to myself yet.

Regardless of what it was, when Zach looked over at me and asked if we could make a quick stop before heading home, I was caught off guard. It was nearing one o'clock in the morning, and in a couple of minutes most places would be closed. However, he parked outside of a local dance club and shared with me that he had been practicing learning how to dance. He said that he would really like to know if he was getting any good. I hesitated at first, making excuses that the club would be closing soon, but he gently encouraged me, sharing that it was just one dance.

Just.

One.

Dance.

That was all it took. He was good. At dancing, I mean. And as his body was in tune with the slow music, our bodies stayed together—close together—in unison, with his strong arms around me I felt like I was melting into them. My heart began to heat up, and my body softened to his touch. This feeling that I had been avoiding for so long was now unavoidable as we circled each other. And as his warm breath lingered on my cheek while he towered over me, I began to feel pieces of my wall crumbling, each bit of eye contact shaking the thick layer of bricks around my heart.

Something was happening.

My wall still existed, but the blocks had been moved and nothing felt stable anymore.

My feelings had been built on a tower of bricks that Zach was someone else's "That Man," but not mine. That's why I opened up to him. That's why I called him out on his frailties. That's why I felt a security and freedom in his presence. I had always told myself that Zach wasn't dateable, which, to me, meant that sharing my truest self wouldn't push him away.

But something was happening now, and the cracks in my wall were now holes.

I left that night unsure of what I was feeling, unsure of what was happening, and desperately needing to talk to God.

And so that's what I did.

Where do you want me, Lord? And what do you want me to do with this whole Zach situation? Lord, he is a great guy, and I have a lot of fun hanging out with him, but … he's not MY great guy! Father, guard his heart, and I pray for our friendship. I also pray for "That Man." I pray that You would lay me on his heart and make him pursue me. I pray that I would meet him soon and that You, Oh God, would direct our path. Thank you, Lord!

I left that conversation with God trusting that He would answer my prayer, even if I was unsure how He would do it. However, I also felt like the tower that I had built was shaking a bit. I wasn't sure what was next, how I should approach these new feelings that developed, and so I did what felt natural, what felt safe. I placed those bricks back where they came from, plugging up those holes, those feelings, and going back to life as usual.

Or so I thought.

It was the second weekend in April, and just a few weeks had gone by since Zach had taken me dancing. Life felt just like it had prior to that night. Work was going well, our Bible study group continued to meet and enjoy time together, and my relationship with Zach felt the same as it had before. To be honest, after that night, he and I didn't really talk about the dance. He was still a good friend, we continued to hang out in groups, and I still liked having him around.

I did not want things to change. I didn't want my feelings to change. I didn't want my thoughts to change. But the main thing was that I didn't want to feel out of control. Despite the fact that I believed that the Lord would take care of me, I still had some lingering feelings about Zach, and that made me uncomfortable. I wanted to protect myself from falling into something that God didn't want for me, so I decided that the best way to protect myself was to do things on my terms. See Zach on my terms. Talk to him on my terms. Then I would have control. Then I would feel safe.

And then, just like that, it all changed.

As I was babysitting for a couple that lived a few miles from Zach's place, this little three-year-old boy totally pulled his pants down to pee in the grass as I was trying to teach him to play golf. I couldn't stop giggling as it reminded me of Zach's story of him going pantsless on the golf course. As if I couldn't control the compulsion, after I left their house, I jumped in my car and got on my cell phone—he had to hear what happened!

"Hey, I've got a funny story to tell you," I said. "Hello?" I looked down at the screen—my phone battery had died. I had been to Zach's place before, so I decided to stop by and tell him myself. He was going to laugh so hard!

Pulling up to the driveway, I hopped out of the car and ran to the door, giggling to myself about the story I was about to tell. It only took about three or four knocks, but when he opened the door, time seemed to stand still.

He answered, but as he did, all I could notice was that he was shirtless.

Shirtless and in pajama pants.

Shirtless and tan.

Shirtless and well-defined.

My eyes couldn't help but look, and my mind didn't stop me. I just stared at him for a few seconds before shaking my brain back into my head.

"I'm sorry to just stop by, I um … just was … going to finish telling you that story that I called you about …" I stammered.

"Oh Leanne," he said nervously. "I'm glad you stopped by, but," he looked toward the other room as he continued, "the thing is that Hailee stopped by and was real upset, so … she's in the other room."

I stood there stunned for a moment.

Hailee, his ex-girlfriend was there. And Zach was half dressed. My mind did the math quickly and came out with only one conclusion. They were together and they were more than just friends. In an instant, I could feel my emotions flip, catching me entirely off guard.

This whole time I had told him we were friends; I had made it clear that there was nothing between us. I had plans for God to bring me That Man not That Zach. And yet here I was, my feelings, which even the strongest walls could not hold in, were all over the front door stoop of Zach's house. I was jealous. And I felt like a fool.

And now I was angry at myself, and I had to get out of there.

He could see it in my eyes, me trying to hold myself together, but I quickly spat, "I'm so stupid. I should not have come over. I'm sorry, I've got to go!"

I scrambled back into my car, avoiding both eye contact and the stammered words that were coming out of his mouth. He said that he could explain. He said that it wasn't what it looked like. But I didn't want an explanation. I didn't want to hear it. I just wanted to leave.

So I did. I drove away. I drove for hours, only knowing that I didn't want to go back to my apartment, that I didn't want to be found, that I didn't want to show my feelings, that I didn't want to get hurt.

I had to think.

I had to be prepared.

I had to protect myself.

And I knew in those moments that I had to shove those bricks back in their place.

Fourteen
Brick by Brick

Grace upon grace ...
—*John 1:16 (New American Bible)*

I COULDN'T GET THE IMAGE OUT OF MY HEAD: Zach. Shirtless. It played like a video on endless repeat.

Zach. Shirtless.

Zach. Shirtless. Hailee. Repeat.

I felt so much confusion, so much disappointment in myself, so much anger.

But where was all of this emotion coming from? He was my friend. That was it. At least that is what I told myself every day. I told *him* this every day. And I meant it.

Or at least ... I thought I meant it.

I drove around for hours trying to compose myself. Trying to shake these feelings that were swirling around inside of me like a torrential storm. I just needed to get *back*. Back behind my bricks, back behind safety, back behind the wall I had built for myself to keep all of this from happening.

Deep breath in.

Deep breath out.

In. Out. In. Out. In. Out.

And, one breath at a time, I began to find my way back.

It was fine. Everything was fine. I was overreacting. He was just my friend.

Zach didn't do anything wrong. Zach was single. Zach is allowed to be with whomever he wants.

Zach. Shirtless. Hailee. Repeat.

I sat in my car outside our apartment, tears streaming down my face, wondering what had just happened. And that's when I saw him: Zach, with his shirt on, sitting at my front door, twirling his car keys around his fingers under the single overhead light. I felt the night air gently blow across my face as I approached him.

"Zach?" I quietly whispered, wondering if he was even able to hear me at all.

"Leanne," he said, as he jumped to his feet. "I'm so sorry, but I need to talk to you. I need to explain."

And despite everything I had felt hours before, in the cool of the night, standing outside my apartment door, I let him talk.

He told me about how Hailee had just found out that her parents were getting a divorce and she was upset and needed to talk. "She called and asked if she could come over and she was crying and I didn't know what to do ... so I said okay. That's all it was. Nothing else was going on."

And yet, even as the words were coming out of his mouth, I could only picture one thing: Zach. Shirtless. Hailee. Repeat.

And then with more feeling than I anticipated, I shouted, "But you were half dressed, Zach. Shirtless. So you were comfortable enough to be shirtless with her."

At that comment, Zach tore his shirt off, letting it drop to the ground beside him. "And now I'm shirtless with you. Because I'm comfortable enough to be shirtless with *you*."

No more words.

Just Zach. Shirtless.

It was hard to describe what I was feeling right then. Was it the thrill of seeing him shirtless? Or was it the thrill that he effortlessly bared himself, and his feelings, to me? Either way, I was speechless, which gave him the space to explain his side of the situation. After finding my voice, I apologized for reacting the way that I did, for letting my emotions take the reins. What I really meant, though, was that I was sorry I had stepped out from behind my wall, that I had let my guard down for a moment and let myself be seen.

While Zach and I fell back into our normal routine, this time felt different. I was a bit quieter, and he was a bit more distant. We would see each other at Bible study and chat in passing, as though nothing had really happened. I tucked my feelings away, and he was cautious about bringing it up. He would often leave little notes on my windshield when he'd pass my car, and despite missing the closeness of his friendship, I continued to stand tall in my resolve that I had simply been carried away in a momentary wave of emotion. In my own way, though, I was actually grateful to him. Grateful for reminding me why I needed my wall in the first place—because I was determined to never be the other woman ever again. And as the days passed since I saw him with Hailee, I started to realize where all of these angry feelings were actually coming from: Spencer.

But how?

I had left Spencer and all of that mess behind when I moved to Denton. I had grown and healed and spent three years becoming the person I had always hoped to be. The Lord had changed me and forgiven me and given me a safe place to land.

Why now? Why here?

And as I sat on my couch, furiously scribbling out words on paper, the Lord gave me my answer: because he is part of your story.

I shook my head as I stared at the page, almost as though I was trying to erase the thought from my mind.

No. No, he isn't. The experience is not a part of me. I left it.

But it was. And at some point in time, I was going to have to accept it, because while we always have the power to change our stories, we don't have the power to erase them. And regardless of how much I wanted my experience with Spencer to be gone ... the truth is that we all have our histories. They shape us, they teach us, and they guide us.

I have my own history.

Zach has his.

And those histories have led us here, changing us for the better.

But only if we let them.

Seeing Zach with Hailee brought back every awful feeling I had ever had during my time with Spencer. My feelings of hurt, my feelings of insecurity, my feelings of shame. In a single moment of disjointed information, I had been thrown right back to a time and place that I never wanted to see again.

Then came the fear.

The fear that it was all happening again, and the fear that I would lose control.

But was it actually happening again?

This was the question I found myself facing, and it's the question that many of us will face as our fears come rolling through.

Will we let our past keep us from our future? Or will we trust our God to keep writing the story, with grace upon grace?

As I gently sat with all of these questions, one thing became very clear: my feelings for Zach were real. I may have fought against them, and I may have spoken words to deny them, but they were real. History and all, I very much cared for this man. History and all, I believe that he very much cared for me. We may have individually struggled through our past to walk down a road that we didn't plan on traveling, but those roads were behind us now.

What lay ahead was up to us.

Just two weeks after I allowed Hailee's presence to shatter my sense of security, our entire Bible study group (minus James) received an invitation from Zach to join him at his place to make preparations for James's upcoming birthday. Of course, not wanting to miss such an occasion, I let Zach know that I would be there. But when I arrived on the night of the get-together, an hour later than intended, I was the only one there; alone with Zach, at his place, and nothing but the energy of the past few weeks lingering between us.

"No one else showed up?" I asked, glancing around the living room.

"Nope," he grinned. "I guess it's just the two of us!"

If nothing else, Zach was always so great at making me feel comfortable and dissolved any tension with his kind and sweet presence. He always felt like the calm in an otherwise thunderous storm. And so we planned. We baked a cake and made a card and laughed during the moments in between. Just like all the days before.

At around nine p.m. that night, I knew I needed to head home as I had a long day ahead of me the next morning. However, a giant storm had rolled through the area while we were busy laughing, and as much as I needed to rest up, I also didn't want to get drenched trying to make it to my car. Zach and I stood on his porch, debating whether or not I could run between the raindrops, when a blazing lightning bolt made its way across the sky, and the thunder that followed startled me into taking a frightened jump forward. A jump right into Zach's arms. And with his hands gently around my waist, we were now face-to-face. Not just with each other, but with every unspoken word we had never shared with each other. With the rain pouring down around us, our heads leaned in a bit closer. Zach cautiously kissed me, and as we both paused in that stillness, permission was granted. Time stood still.

Fear slipped away.

Walls crashed down.

And my red umbrella of faith had been drawn above the two of us.

I woke up the next morning and just let my body lay heavy on my bed. I couldn't stop thinking about

the rain,

the porch,

the kiss.

Anytime I closed my eyes, I could feel it all over again, and something about it made my stomach twist inside. Despite telling myself that we were just friends, I had dreamt about this closeness with him ever since our dance together. Feeling his hand around my waist, his body so close to mine, the warmth of his breath—all of it was amazing. However, I was still left feeling vulnerable and hesitant and a bit afraid. Like a baby animal needing to step gently out into the light, I knew I needed to step slowly or I would quiver back in fear from the brightness of it all. I was also acutely aware of the fact that I had just broken the rules of the Bible study, and this felt unsettling to me. My emotions had been so stirred up over the last few weeks that I needed a bit of time and space to get my bearings again. So I wrote Zach a letter explaining how I felt and requesting that we not see each other until the end of Bible study, which was another two weeks away.

And in the grand tradition that is Zach, he wrote his own words in return. Words that would carry me through this space of confusion and uncertainty.

Leanne,

    I want you to know that I will seek God every day, pray for you every day, and keep you close to my heart every day.

    Leanne, you are so worth the wait.

    In May, I will be waiting for you.

    No, in May, I'll be pursuing you.

    This is my marathon. I will finish this race. I will be running. Chasing after you.

From ME

And with that, I took my space. A space that left me filled with both excited anticipation and anxious uncertainty. This is what I had always wanted: to have someone reach their hand out for me and never let go. I called and God answered. He brought me a man that would meet me where I stood, that would catch me when I fell, that would love me when I ran. He brought me a man that was just like Him.

Filled with grace upon grace.

On the night of May 3, our Bible study group gathered at my apartment for one final gathering. We ate and we laughed and we reminisced about the year we had just shared together. At one point, I looked around the room and felt this sense of sadness come over me as I realized that it was all over. We had shared so much together and grown so much together. It was an odd feeling to say goodbye. But I also had an excitement building in me about the new possibilities that lay ahead. Zach had respected my request for space over the last two weeks. He was polite and kind, as he always was, but he had kept his distance in a way that felt oddly noticeable. But his letter had left me wondering about what came next, and

I thought there was a possibility that I would soon find out. I was taken aback, though, as our final night together came and went without much contact from Zach. He remained at arm's length throughout our gathering and gave no indication of wanting to pursue otherwise. One by one, as each person left, I waited for him to say something, to close the gap that stood between us. But he didn't. He shared in our stories and helped to clean up, and when everyone started to leave, he said his goodbyes and walked out of my apartment door.

He was gone.

As the last person left, I walked around my apartment in a state of mild internal panic. I could hear Lindsay chattering in the background as she recapped about the highlights of the evening, and meanwhile I simply wandered aimlessly, putting dishes in the sink and gathering chip bowls from the other room. I couldn't help but wonder if I had missed something, if my chance had passed me by, if That Man had just walked out the door for good.

I could feel the anxiety rise within me.

Part of me wanted to just step back behind my wall where it was safe, but there was no wall anymore.

As I grabbed a couple of half-filled glasses off our dining room table, I noticed something from the corner of my eye. It was Zach's keys and wallet. They were still here, and there was no way that he was going to get very far without them. Just as I went to reach for them, I heard a knock at the door.

My breathing halted, and my heart began to race.

I walked toward the door, slowly opening it toward me.

"Hi Leanne," he said, with a smile that was both charming and mischievous. "I seem to have forgotten something ..."

Fifteen
Jericho

I always thank my God for you because
of his grace given you in Christ.

—1 Cor. 1:4 (NIV)

I HAVE ALWAYS LOVED THE STORY OF JERICHO IN THE BIBLE. It's a story about a man's trust in God and how that trust led him to victory, to a deeply rich life, and to his true purpose.

This story is about a man named Joshua and his battle against the Canaanites. The Canaanites lived in the city of Jericho, a place that was seen as one of great pleasures, enjoying an abundance of food, water, and seeming safety. However, the people who lived in the land of Canaan were not followers of God. Because of this, God ordered the Israelites, Joshua's people, to destroy Jericho. They were to take down the wall that surrounded the city of Jericho, a wall that was said to be impenetrable, to simply walk around it for six days, and on the seventh day, with a loud trumpet blast, the wall would crash, showing God's ultimate power and sovereignty. Joshua was a man who had a battle to fight and, rather than relying on his own understanding, he simply obeyed God, even if it required an uncomfortable amount of trust, time, and patience.

Six days of silent marching. Six days of waiting. Joshua didn't understand all of the details of God's best plan, but he believed that in the end, if he just trusted, if he just listened, God would help bring him to his promised land, breaking down the wall that kept in it his future, his destiny.

And that seventh day—the day when they cried out in obedience, the day when the trumpets blasted at God's command—that was the day when the wall came crashing down. That was the day when victory came.

• • •

My eyes were fixed on Zach, and I could feel my heart beating outside my chest as those words came out of his mouth. I attempted to gain my footing and to not show him on the outside all of the feelings I was having on the inside. I knew he wouldn't have been able to go far without his keys and his wallet, but I could feel a nervousness that I hadn't felt in a long, long time. I liked him. I really liked him. And I was glad he came back.

I swung his keys back and forth on my finger as we stood together at the doorway to my apartment, our eyes locked on one another. "I didn't know if you were going to talk to me tonight."

"Oh Leanne, it's no accident that I left my keys here. Come outside, I really want to talk to you."

The sun had fallen in the sky and, with it, the warm Texas heat, giving way to cooler night air and crystal-clear skies. It felt like God caused the stars to sparkle just for us as we sat on the tailgate of his Toyota 4Runner, one of our favorite spots to have conversations. As I stared at my feet, I could feel him looking at me, I could feel his smile widen. Lifting my chin to meet his gaze, he expressed how he had been praying for this day, that he wanted to take our relationship further, and now that the Bible study was over, he would like to take me on a real date.

He waited for me.

He pursued me.

He prayed, he trusted, and he was persistent.

He sought after God, and now he was seeking after me

During the past two weeks—the two weeks where I had asked for space—I had come to the realization that life was just not quite the same without Zach in it. I wanted to share the funny things with him, the sad things with him, the hard things with him—I wanted to share life with my best friend. That was it. But that wasn't all. There was more. More to my feelings. More to my desire. More. I had feelings for him. Strong feelings for him. And this awakening over the past two weeks surprised me. Now this wall I was attempting to rebuild didn't feel quite right anymore. Those old walls, the ones I had built around my heart, had begun to shake a little over the last few months. God had plans for those walls to come down. He had made a way with my best friend. He had made a way with Zach. And just like He did for Joshua and the Israelites, God wanted to see victory in my life.

And so, right there, in what felt like the most perfect of moments, I said yes to our first date.

Just three days after our talk on the tailgate, Zach was at my apartment door again, this time with a handful of roses and a note attached with the now treasured words "From Me." I could feel his love, as he looked at me with those deep blue eyes, kissing my cheek and whispering, "You are so beautiful, Leanne."

Our first date was to a dinner theater in Dallas, something that I will remember forever because while it was super fun, it also had an element of discomfort. Which, let's be honest, most good dates have.

After dinner, this sweet older couple standing next to us commented on our playful flirting.

"Oh, look how sweet," the woman said. "Can we have an invitation to your wedding?"

I remember feeling a shock of awkwardness, given that we were only on our first date, but Zach laughed, politely acknowledged them, and with his hand on the small of my back, guided me outside. I remember thinking that despite the uneasiness of that moment, I was so happy to be here with him—here with my best friend, here with someone who knew me so intimately—that I didn't need to pretend. I didn't need to be something or someone that I was not. This was my comfort zone, with Zach by my side and no walls in between us.

The truth was that this was a learning experience for me. Not really in my relationship with Zach but rather in my understanding of God, His love for us, and His ultimate plan and purpose. Dating had been a challenge throughout my young life. It was filled with secrets, shame, uncertainty, isolation, and confusion. With Zach, however, dating seemed effortless, and all of my life experiences were enhanced with fun, comfort, and joy.

It was as if my prayers as a young girl, my prayers for the perfect man who would sweep me off of my feet, had finally been presented to me. God was giving me a gift with Zach. God knew what He was doing. And I remember thinking to myself, *Wow, God, you gave me this. You gave me a person who sees me, knows me, and cares for me. You did this! And I'm so glad it was Your plan and not mine.*

I would say that this story with Zach began as the school year was coming to an end, but honestly I believe our story began before I was aware that there was even a story between us. The Bible study during that year was from the Lord. It was not only the place for learning and fellowship, but it was also the space that God carved out for me to meet Zach.

A safe place for my heart. And as I felt the intensity of my relationship with Zach increase, I could feel some of the other relationships I had prayed for slip away.

Looking back, I can see how the Bible study group taught me so much about my own expectations. I believed at the time that I knew what God was doing with that study. That I was there to use my gifts and my past to help younger girls see God's grace. I believed in the beginning that my faithful God was bringing me That Man by putting James and I together in that Bible study. In fact, I was so sure of it! I believed I could see God's plan for me, but in His wisdom and timing, I instead gained the beautifully unexpected.

There was something so natural about it all with Zach and me. He was my best friend, and putting a label on the two of us as a couple only enhanced the already solid relationship we had. Other than losing the community of our Bible study at year's end, things pretty much stayed the same. We still spent time hanging out with some of the same people, enjoying each other's company, and living life together.

As Zach and I spent more time together, we also had family and friends intertwine more and more in our everyday life. I had dinner with Zach's family a few times and got to know his three brothers. Their comical and sometimes crazy stories would have my side in a stitch for hours. My family also welcomed Zach with open arms, and their affection for him grew quickly. My dad was won over by Zach's willingness to join in on each recreational undertaking thrown at him. If Zach was good to me and willing to golf, ski, fish, and work, then my dad gave Zach the seal of approval. And because my mom knew all about my three-year commitment, she was sold on God's plan for Zach and me to be together.

Everything was so natural, so fun with Zach. I mean really, truly, fun. I remember one time specifically, during a torrential Texas rainstorm, we had been standing under the porch at my apartment watching the rain pour down, when Zach looked over at me with that twinkle in his eye, the look that meant some idea was brewing.

"What if we drive up to North Lakes Park and turn the whole soccer field into one giant muddy slip 'n' slide?" he suggested with childlike glee.

Throwing caution to the wind, I grabbed an old pair of tennis shoes, tossed my hair up in a ponytail, and quickly ran between surges of rain into the passenger seat of his 4Runner. When we arrived at the field, it was as if the rain had started to fall more steadily just for us. It felt as if God was joining in on the fun. And so, with reckless abandon, we scrambled out of the car and dove headfirst, over and over again, onto the saturated field, covering our clothes with earth and muck and our hearts with laughter. To most, this rain was just a part of a normal Texas summer storm, but for me this moment was a confirmation of another blessing from heaven. God knew I had asked for rain before. He knew I had been praying for That Man. And now he gave me both.

Zach was full of exciting adventures, but he also continued to surprise me with his ambitions and maturity. I had to at times remind myself that he was only twenty-one years old. He was forward-thinking and intentional—unlike most guys I had encountered in their early twenties. He still had one year left of college before he graduated, but he had moved out of his parents' house, he continued to hold down two jobs, and he was now leading a guys' Bible study over the summer. The Bible student had become the teacher. The boy had become a man. And it honestly impressed me.

He also impressed my friends. I still remember a conversation I had with my girlfriends one Friday night about how my relationship with Zach was a gift from God. Over popcorn and ice cream, I spilled my heart out to my closest friends, Whitney, Kee, and Lindsay. I shared how I had never felt this way before and that, for the first time in my life, I could say that I truly believed that he was the man I was supposed to marry.

But as I talked, my heart ached for those three words to reverberate in the air around me. *I love you.* He never uttered them to me, and, boy, I sure wished he would.

As I voiced my pain, the realization of my own dogmatic statements made to Lindsay only a few months prior came to my recollection. I remembered that, with Zach's listening ears in the room, I told her with utter certainty that no one should talk about marriage until there's a ring. That no one should talk about love until there's a ring. That no one should talk about a ring until there's a ring. And at that moment I felt like a walking contradiction. I could see now that my pride had bit me in the butt, that it had been keeping me from hearing those very words from Zach.

After apologizing again to Lindsay over my poorly thought-out (and poorly timed) comment, Whitney piped up: "Well, if he doesn't say I love you—what does he say? *I like you?*"

"Go get some of the notes Zach has given you," Lindsay said, nudging me to my room.

The four of us dug through a shoebox filled with letters I had collected from Zach, notes that acknowledged me and made me feel like a princess being swept off her feet.

"I adore you more and more every day," Kee read and pretended to swoon.

"You are so precious to me—a treasure and a sweet gift

from God," Whitney read and held the letter to her chest.

"I'm head-over-heels crazy about you," I whispered as my smile grew.

"Oh my gosh, Leanne, if you don't marry him, I will!" Lindsay gushed.

As we read Zach's words of affirmation to me, I realized that I not only had someone in my life that would share his feelings about me, but I also had friends to share these moments with. The four of us giggled as we poured over these notes that were Zach's way of telling me he loved me, and honoring my hardheadedness, using every word but "love" and "marriage."

Soon the calendar neared the middle of June, marking time for me to leave on a mission trip to Venezuela with my church. I hadn't been anticipating a whirlwind romance when I first signed up for this trip, and now I was caught up in the heat of it all. Zach and I had been inseparable, and now time and space would separate us for a few weeks, giving me time to reflect on all that God had given me in him. I felt a confirmation in my heart that he was "That Man" before leaving, but God, in his perfect way, used this trip to give me an even deeper understanding of His love for me and the gift of Zach in my life.

On the second day, I opened my Bible and found a letter placed at Psalm 96. In Zach's perfect handwriting, he wrote, "Sing to the Lord a new song."

He wrote those beautiful words to encourage me that I had a new song to sing and to share my story with those in Venezuela. I sighed and brought the paper to my chest. He was part of my new song and part of my new story, and I wished he was with me so I could show those around me how good God was. Even though I wanted to thank him, Zach and

I could not communicate during my trip. No phone calls. No emails. Nothing. I missed him. I adored him. I wanted him.

As my plane landed on Texas soil, my heart felt as if it was going to hop out of my chest in anticipation of seeing Zach. And as I scanned the crowd at the airport, my eyes found his, filling my body with a heat that had only intensified over time. And as though my body couldn't contain it any longer, my feet ran to him of their own volition.

"Zach!" I cried, as I almost knocked him down in a hug.

"So you did miss me!" he joked as I smothered him with part of my hair and carry-on backpack.

"Well, you are my ride home," I laughed.

The air between us was so electric, it could have lit a lightbulb. I didn't want to let go of his hand. I didn't want to be separated from him when I got in the passenger side of the car. Even as he drove home, he grabbed my hand so we could still have contact.

"Hey, I know you have many things to catch up on after your trip, but I was wondering if you could carve out some time for me this Saturday. I want you all to myself."

"Yes," I said with a smile. "I'd love to."

"Be ready by six a.m.," he said, slamming the trunk shut and hauling my luggage inside. "Oh, and bring your purse and your Bible."

"Six a.m.? What are we going to do so early in the morning?"

"We're going to get breakfast at a fun little place with spectacular views."

Sixteen
The Dream

> And the grace of our Lord was exceedingly
> abundant, with faith and love.
>
> —*1 Tim. 1:14 (NKJV)*

B EFORE THE SUN WAS UP ON SATURDAY MORNING, I sat next
to my apartment window, staring out into the dark, and
I couldn't help but think about all the parts of my life—all
the moments—that I *needed* to go through so that I could be
here. The hard ones, the shame-filled ones, the distant and
confused ones. The dark moments before the sunrise. And
unless you have been waiting prayerfully and patiently for
that ball of yellow to break the horizon, the everyday miracle of that moment when the sun breaks the horizon can
get lost. But that day all I was doing at that moment was
waiting for my boyfriend to pick me up for breakfast. And
yet it seemed to have God painted all over it. A masterpiece
that even I couldn't have anticipated.

Promptly, at six a.m., Zach pulled up in front of my building, and with his signature smile he greeted me at the door.
After spending more time apart than we had ever experienced
before, this day together was exactly what I needed. To connect, to join hands, to fill my soul with the wonder of this
man that I had the gift of knowing. When Zach mentioned
fantastic views earlier in the week, I considered the possibility
of a day filled with adventure and fun, somewhere in the
Texas landscape. But as we drove down the highway, farther

from the wide-open spaces, I began to question him on exactly *where* we were headed for breakfast.

Zach just smiled and said coyly, "It's a surprise!"

The parking garage was still so dark and filled with early morning risers unloading their luggage and quietly seeking their destinations. I glanced around and my heart began to pump quickly. Why were we at the airport?

Zach pulled into a spot close to the terminal, put the 4Runner in park, and looked over at me with excited anticipation.

"Leanne, I want to take you to New York. Feel like hopping on a plane to come and see it with me?"

I clapped my hands and threw open the door. If I could have taken a day trip to anywhere in the world, it would have been there! Even as surprised as I was, a part of me also wasn't surprised at all. Because if Zach had taught me anything, he had taught me that life with him would be full of surprises. And that this was only just the beginning. I jumped out of my seat like a kid on Christmas morning, and it was all I could do to not race him to the terminal. Zach quickly snatched his backpack from the bed of the truck, then promptly put my hand in his, and it was this moment, as the sun made its first appearance, that I knew this was going to be the brightest sunrise.

Once we boarded the plane and plopped down in our seats, Zach turned toward me and said, "This is just what I wanted today to be; just me and you."

"So, do you have anything special planned for us today?" I questioned.

"Nope, no plans," he stated, "In fact, the day is all yours. Why don't you make a list of all the things you want to do, and we'll see how many we can get done in six hours."

Bummer, I thought. This would be a great opportunity to

get engaged. But it's not a good idea for me to get my hopes up. So as I argued with myself about Zach's motives, I realized that no matter what we would do that day, I wanted to be in this moment with him.

God has never rushed a single moment of my blessed story. He certainly wasn't going to start now.

We landed in New York a little after eleven a.m. to the most beautiful summer weather. The skies were clear and the air was warm but still much cooler than July in Texas. We immediately flagged down a cab and jumped in.

"Fifth Avenue and West Fifty-Ninth Street, please—Pulitzer Plaza," Zach told the driver.

"I thought you said we had no plans. That address is pretty specific," I said, nudging him with my shoulder.

"You said you wanted to go to Central Park, so let's go there first."

One thing I knew about Zach is that even though he was spontaneous with his adventures, he was also always prepared.

A sea of yellow cabs spread out before us, and towering buildings and beautiful burrows enveloped us on every side. The driver dropped us off near Central Park, and as soon as we arrived, I remember feeling an overload of sensory detail—the cars, the crowded streets filled with businessmen, and the women running to grab their lunch from their favorite food cart. Then as we turned the corner, I could see the color of the dark green leaves of the pear trees popping against the gray buildings that seemed to grow out of the concrete for miles. The morning workday rush had calmed to make way for the sightseers and casual strollers to walk at their leisure.

Then rising up right in front of me was a beautiful stone

fountain against the backdrop of the Plaza Hotel. The stream cascaded from the top fountain tier to the second and third into the massive pool with water the color of juniper.

"Come on, let's sit over here. I'd like to talk to you for a little bit before we start our day of sightseeing," he said as he placed his hand on my back, leading me to the bench formed from the fountain's wall. We sat, then he wiped his hands on the sides of his pants and pulled out a piece of paper from his pocket. "Leanne, I have a letter I would like to read to you. I wrote it all down so I wouldn't forget."

I nodded, feeling my stomach do somersaults of excitement.

"Leanne, I can't believe how good God is. To be where I am today is all Him. His plan and timing is perfect. I remember back in November I had to stand on my tiptoes looking over a wall. I saw a girl who had given her heart away—she put it in a safe place. In this girl I saw Christ. I saw her true love. I saw her focus. I began to pray that God would give me an incredible gift. A gift that I do not deserve. I prayed for your heart. I prayed to God to trust me with it. I want, I desire, your heart."

And as those words showered me like a gentle loving rain, he bent down on one knee and slowly took a ring out of his pocket—a ring that symbolized his love for me before today, now, and in the future. And this three-stone princess cut was the most beautiful ring I had ever seen.

"Leanne, you are my best friend. You make me whole. I can't imagine my life without you. And I don't want to. I love you! Will you marry me?"

"Yes! Yes! Yes!" I said with tears streaming down my face.

Standing, Zach quickly swept me into his arms, swinging me around and pressing his lips against mine, his hands moving from my waist to the small of my back, our breath mingled perfectly together in space.

And for the briefest of moments, in the city that never sleeps, there was no one but us.

He then stepped back with the biggest grin on his face and looked around. "I JUST GOT ENGAGED!" Zach yelled and threw his hands up in the air.

And right then, this crowd of people, who were all busy with her own lives, with places to go and people to see, clapped and cheered for us.

They celebrated us and they took in the moment *with* us. They lifted us up with their love and encouragement, complete strangers who had now become a part of our story.

And it was like a dream. A dream bigger than I could have ever imagined—it was *The Dream*. The dream I'd had since I was a little girl with a red spiral notebook filled with hopes and wishes for That Guy. The dream where I could see "the Grace of [my] Lord was exceedingly abundant, with faith and love" (1 Tim. 1:14, NKJV). The dream where I prayed for my prince to come and he would lock eyes with me and know that I was his.

And as I stood there, in my very own fairy tale, I had never felt more loved and showered with God's abounding grace. For all that I had done and all the directions I had gone, I was still forgiven. More importantly, I always had been. While I may have left God at times, He had never left me.

At the end of our day trip, after we ate New York–style pizza, got lost in Times Square, kissed along Fifth Avenue, and went to the top of the Empire State Building, this amazing adventure felt like a beautiful pause in time. Until it was time to rush back to the airport. Fueled entirely off of adrenaline and romance, we booked it back to the terminal.

On the flight home, there was just "us," sitting side by side, headed in the direction of our dreams together. We had arrived in New York as two people in love. We were leaving New York as two people starting a whole new chapter of our lives together.

"Here's a gift for you," Zach said as he handed me a rustic brown journal delicately tied with a thin piece of leather string.

"What's this?" I asked, feeling the soft leather in my hands.

"I started writing in this back in November. Three days after you and I played basketball during our retreat. Read it," he said with a twinkle in his eyes.

I grinned, then looked down at this perfect book that belonged to that man I loved. Slowly, I opened the cover of the worn journal, my awareness leaving the confines of the plane and entering into the pages of Zach's story:

The Bible study retreat was this past weekend. Once I came home, I immediately went to the store to look for a journal—a journal to start writing to you. Because my goal, Leanne, is to give you this journal when I propose.

... You understand me, you understand grace, and you understand forgiveness.

... I want to send you flowers, but I don't want to freak you out, so I have a plan. I'm not going to sign my name. Instead I am hoping to be around for a long time, and I pray that whenever you get flowers they are always from me.

... At your party after the retreat, when I said, "I had never been in love," that would have been true just fifteen days ago. I fell in love with you on that concrete driveway playing basketball in Graham, and though I knew you before the retreat, it was like I was struck by lightning that day. It's like I loved you on that day,

and every day after I have fallen deeper and deeper in love with you.

I met your friend Kee at a dance party college life was having. I pulled her aside and told her I wanted her to teach me how to dance because I wanted to dance with a special person, and I wanted to make sure I was good. She asked me who I wanted to dance with, and I wasn't sure if I should tell her or not, but I wanted to . . . so I did. She was great and told me to go for it . . .

. . . It feels just like a movie to me when I am with YOU. You are in focus while everything else is blurry. When I'm with you, I can't see anything else. I admire and respect your trust of the Lord and your faithfulness.

. . . Today you made me laugh so hard my side hurt.

Lucky day—well for me, I guess. I saw you walking home from school and realized that your car needed a jump. I always want to be the one to save the day for you, and here was my first opportunity! Once your car started and you smiled at me, I thought my heart would pop. You really have no idea how much you and your smile brighten my day. Not only that, while we were drinking hot chocolate, you told me straight to my face to pay off my credit cards. I like that you don't mess around—you just say it like it is. It is so nice to know that I can tell you anything.

You make me want to be a better man.

We went with a group to see a movie today, but you made me sit by Mia. I know what you are trying to do, but you have no idea how crazy I am about you.

I was blown away by you and your care for Lindsay after her boyfriend broke up with her. BUT you know what else I found out? You DO NOT want to talk about marriage until there is a ring. That's fine with me, be-cause believe me—there will be a ring.

... I always want to be the one to take care of you.

... I then went on to tell your brother's friend that I was going to marry you one day. Then he laughed and said that that was a bold statement. I said I have never been more sure of anything in my life.

... The thing that you don't know is that when I in-vited everyone in the Bible study to come help with the birthday planning and make a card for James, I was really just waiting to see if you would come. And once you said that you were coming—I called and told every-one else that I moved it to tomorrow. I'm so glad I had you all to myself.

I truly don't feel the Lord telling me "no" in pursu-ing you. In fact, I feel it's a strong "yes"!

I'm continuing to pray for us daily. I have told the Lord that I will pursue you in May, and if we are not meant to be, then the answer you give me when I ask will be the "yes" or "no" for us. I've never felt like this before, and I miss you so much. And it's not just be-cause I want to take this relationship to the next step, but it's because I miss my friend.

... The couple next to us asked if they could have an invitation to our wedding! I tried so hard to play it cool, but inside I was as giddy as a kid on Christmas morning. All I wanted to say was, "Sure, write down your address and I'll send you one as soon as I can!" But be-fore that, step one. First Date. Check that one off my list.

I asked you this question today. "If you could go anywhere for just one day, where would you go?" Do you remember what you said? You said, "New York City."

Well, I've got a plan. And I've talked to Kee about it. I can't wait, Leanne.

We went to Graham today, and I loved getting to be around your family more and more. I really enjoy spending time with your parents and Marcus. I love how fun it is to be with you and your family. It just makes me happy. I also love how close you all are and how much you love and support each other.

You left today on a mission trip to Venezuela. I'm already missing you. I've got two weeks before you get back. But I've got a list of things to get done to keep me busy, one of which includes going with Kee to pick out a ring. She told me the style you like, and so I went to a jewelry store and put a down payment on one they are going to make for you. I know we haven't talked about marriage, but I feel like you would say "yes" now. I knew what I wanted a long time ago. I just had to wait on you to catch up.

. . . I love that God broke down your walls for me.

. . . Went to Graham to talk to your parents today. I was a little nervous, so I had rehearsed the answer to a multitude of questions that I thought your dad might ask me, but when I asked for their blessing, they were both really happy for us. It was funny because the only question your dad asked me was if I wanted to go fishing!

As I read over these journal entries from Zach, I could see his story perfectly intertwining with mine. His days became my days. His story had become my story. He was the answer to my prayer—he was the rain, and all God had asked of me was to hold the umbrella and wait. I had prayed to

God, with faith enough for a desert to flood, that he would pick out the prince for me, but even when I couldn't see it, He already had.

There will never be another moment in my life like the one I experienced that day when Zach asked me to be his wife. There will be so many more moments to come of sheer joy and love and gratitude for the blessings of this incredible story, but this one will forever stand alone as one of the most beautiful chapters of all.

It will stand alone because of how very much we were not alone. Like the fairy tales I loved so much as a child, I had never felt more seen or desired or pursued than I had in this moment. And I don't just mean by Zach, whose heart will never cease to amaze me. The tears that poured out of me that day went beyond the ring on my finger and the strangers we met and the kind gestures made by them.

These tears were for the amazing God who had never left my side.

In the story of our lives, we all have our dragons to slay and our battles to fight. We're all the beautiful princesses, and sometimes we're even the wicked stepsisters. But most importantly, we've all got an unseen hero ready to set us free.

Every fairy tale does.

But what they never tell you in those tales of wonder and romance is that the one who saves us isn't the knight in shining armor.

The one who saves us is the Great King from above.

Because in every story of redemptive love, the King comes first. The prince comes after.

Epilogue

Dear Leanne,

I am learning that life is made up of moments ... small singular moments. And many times, we don't realize the impact of these moments until much later on in life. The days, weeks, and years blur together and then, all of a sudden, these small moments become something much larger.

But occasionally there are moments, incredibly significant ones, when you know right then and there that something special is happening.

I remember a very specific singular moment like it was yesterday. It was a warm November day when I fell in love with a beautiful Jesus-loving girl. I knew from that moment forward, I would love her for the rest of my life, I knew that she would be my wife, and I knew that I would spend the rest of my life pursuing her.

I love telling others how the Lord brought us together—every single time. Recalling our story reminds me of how much I am head-over-heels crazy about you still today.

But please know, I do not want our engagement story to be the highlight—I want the most beautiful part of our story to be me continuing to love and treasure you.

Leanne, you know how we talk about 1 Timothy 6:11

when we do premarital counseling. It says, "pursue love" as if it is very easy to lose. As if it is easy to become sidetracked. As if it is easy to become complacent. While in a relationship, we must be continually pursuing love because marriage is dynamic, it is not static—a marriage either gets better or worse; it does not stay the same. There is a continual effort required of us not to assume we have the "love thing" down. As we live our lives, we must continue to chase after love. If we are not engaged in love, then we could become apathetic, we could become indifferent—which is the opposite of love.

With twenty years of marriage under our belt, the Lord has blessed us with four wonderful boys, photos to fill dozens of scrapbooks, and, Lord willing, stories that we will retell for years to come. We have walked on the mountain tops with God by our side when He brought us Bo as a miracle baby and then three more boys as blessings from above. He has also brought us through the valleys when you had two back surgeries, you could hardly move, and we had to live out our vows in sickness or in health. We experienced these highs and lows in life—but always with each other, hand in hand. My love for you has only grown stronger, and my affections only stirred deeper for you. I truly love you more today than when we first met.

From before we met, you showed your love by praying for "That Man," and you continue to show your love toward me with your daily prayers. I cherish the fact that I have a wife that continues to demonstrate her love for me each and every day. I am so grateful that God joined us together!

I have loved learning more and more about you as if you are new to me each day. You are the most faithful person I know. You hold the hand of God like a small child in perfect peace with your Father. You have a solid foundation of truth that is unwavering. You stand tall in your convictions. Your prayer life is vibrant, and you pray with strong confidence, as if your prayers have already been answered—like the story of the girl filled with faith and her red umbrella. You are teachable—always wanting to better yourself. You are always up for playing a game, of any kind, and are more competitive than you think you are. You make me laugh when you say things out of the blue that are completely unexpected. I love the fact that I know exactly where I stand with you as you can offer a kind rebuke with grace and charity. You are patient with me. You have a fierce devotion to family. You are my best friend. Outside the Holy Spirit, Leanne, you are the greatest gift God has given me.

I want our story to only get better with each passing day. You are not simply a trophy that has been won, but you are my treasure. Leanne, I know in your youth you dreamed of having a fairy-tale story, and my goal for the rest of your life is to make you always feel like *That Girl*.

My Love, I will pursue your heart for as long as I live.

From:
Me

Acknowledgments

This book is a testimony to the love, support, and encouragement of my best friend, *That Man*, my husband—Zach. With
all my heart, thank you, my love, for always being my biggest
fan. You have not only poured out your love for me in time
and resources, but you have done it with a joyful heart. Your
pursuit of Jesus has never wavered, and God continues to use
you in ways that amaze me. You are more than I prayed for all
those years ago, and I'm grateful God's hand put us together.
I look forward to the future—may the pages keep turning and
our eyes stay fixed on Jesus.

Writing this book would not have been possible without all
the friends and family who have built me up and encouraged
me along this road called life. I am a better person because of
the way you loved me and pushed me toward knowing Jesus.

Hugs and more hugs to my parents. Mom, thanks for always being my cheerleader! Your encouragement means the
world to me. Dad, thank you for showing me how to give
with a happy heart, and thank you for making life so fun.

To my boys, who have been my joy and delight. I pray
this story is just the start of a heritage passed down from generation to generation. Pray for *That Girl*, and let's just watch
and see what God will do.

There are times when the words "thank you" don't quite hit the mark of what you are feeling. The words "thank you" are something you say when someone passes the salt across a table or to the checkout person at the grocery store. Thank you doesn't grasp the depths of my gratitude toward these two ladies. Whatever the word would be for my jaw dropping and my cheeks sore from smiling—that's the word I'm looking for. I am so deeply indebted to Genevieve Georget and Malary Hill for their work on this book. Without them to coach me, create beautiful flow, and do master editing, this book would have lacked content, vulnerability, and direction. Thank you for taking my crayon drawings and turning them into a beautiful work of art!

A million "thank-yous" to Sarah Byrd, who feels like family, for using her talents and deep care to make this book better. To Yolanda Knight, a giant bear hug of thanks for holding my hand and encouraging me from beginning to end, and to Sunny and Christy and the entire creative team at RTC, who brought this book to life with their artistry and imagination.

And to you, my reader, thank you for reading this book. It means a great deal to me that you would take the time to hear God's story in my life. I pray we get to meet some day soon.

About the author

Leanne Rozell's life has been shaped by her deep belief in the power of prayer. After experiencing God in mighty ways throughout her life, she learned that when she leaned into God, He would answer her prayers in bigger and better ways than she ever thought possible. Her desire is to leave a legacy of trust in the Lord and to connect with other young people who are struggling to understand the path set before them. Leanne lives in North Texas with her husband and four energetic boys, and it may not always be her pleasure, but it is certainly her duty to be chef, nurse, teacher, and chauffeur. However, she always finds comfort knowing family time is priceless even when it includes painting over marker drawings on the wall.

Made in the USA
Coppell, TX
14 November 2021

65640718R00104